DOCUMENTARY

BOOK

PUBLISHERS

SEATTLE, WASHINGTON

"Let's Go On"

PACIFIC NORTHWEST BALLET AT 25

WAYNE JOHNSON

Page 2: Jeffrey Stanton and Patricia Barker in Pacific
Northwest Ballet's production of George Balanchine's
Chaconne. Photo by Ben Kerns.

COPYRIGHT © 1997

DOCUMENTARY BOOK PUBLISHERS

SEATTLE, WASHINGTON

"Let's Go On":
Pacific Northwest Ballet at 25

Printed in Canada by Hemlock Printers Ltd.
Distributed in the United States by Sasquatch Books
Distributed in Canada by Raincoast Books Ltd.

Author: Wayne Johnson
Editor: Barry Provorse
Copy editor: Sherri Schultz
Cover and interior design: The Leonhardt Group
Production: Paul Langland

Library of Congress Cataloging-in-Publication Data
LC# 97-33586
Johnson, Wayne 1930–
"Let's Go On": Pacific Northwest Ballet at 25
ISBN 0-935503-20-X
1. Pacific Northwest Ballet–History. 2. Ballet companies–Northwest, Pacific–History. I. Title.

Documentary Book Publishers
615 Second Avenue
Seattle, Washington 98104
(206) 467-4300
e-mail: docbooks@sasquatchbooks.com
http://www.sasquatchbooks.com

Documentary Book Publishers publishes books for corporate and institutional clients across North America. For more information about our titles and services, contact us at the address listed above.

Contents

Ballet is important and significant, yes.
But first of all, it is a pleasure.

GEORGE BALANCHINE {1904-1983}

The man who renewed the art of ballet in the mid-20th century by giving it new American energy and flair also said, "I have no literary approach—except to literature." No claim is made that this book is important and significant, let alone literature, but its intent certainly is to share pleasure:

❈ In observing dancers in a rehearsal studio, superbly fit athletes regularly challenging the limits of their bodies and psyches.

❈ In seeing the same dancers on stage, transformed by theatrical lighting, costumes, stylish coiffures and dramatic makeup, creating art that ranges from visceral to ethereal.

❈ In being part of a standing ovation that signals the success of a ballet.

❈ In watching a ballet company build from one success to another until it achieves the stature of a successful institution.

And for those with a taste for *schadenfreude*, there are a company's multiple setbacks, complex problems and failures, to say nothing of the swarming gossip. Ballet, as the old saying goes, is not a matter of life and death; it's more important than that.

Pacific Northwest Ballet in Seattle is celebrating 25 years of achievement by dancing with the guy and gal who brought it: Kent Stowell and Francia Russell, the company's artistic directors for the last 20 years. They, in turn, are continuing to do that which has propelled the company to the top echelon of American ballet companies: they are embracing risk. The latest example is the schedule they put together for PNB's silver anniversary season: a gala retrospective, ten world premieres and four Seattle premieres, including a new full-length work by Kent, *Silver Lining*, set to the music of Jerome Kern.

In the beginning of any ballet or ballet company are the dancers. Both Kent and Francia were soloists in the New York City Ballet during Balanchine's heyday. Their routes to New York were so different that it's surprising they ever met and remarkable that they married—remarkable, that is, only if one dismisses the yin-yang concept. Kent and Francia embody that idea, complementing each other's strengths and weaknesses and constituting the marital equation celebrated by e.e. cummings as "the wonderful one times one."

Francia has sharp features and aristocratic bearing; Kent is soft-featured and casual. She could pass for royalty, he for a one-of-the-guys jokester. Francia's eyes are like a hawk's; she misses nothing. Kent's heavy eyelids suggest a relaxed attitude, but he, too, misses nothing. In the rehearsal studio or on stage, their demeanors are virtually identical. Motionless, they concentrate on the dancers and then move quickly when they detect flaws. Now on their feet, they are clearly the two best mime artists in the company, and although their bodies no longer have the flexibility of youth, their demonstrations of desired movement are precise and graceful.

In rehearsal Kent or Francia signal a halt by sharp hand clapping, and in the following pin-drop quiet, they make their corrections as dancers silently nod in assent. After the necessary adjustments are made, Kent or Francia says: "Let's go on," and music and dance resume. The phrase has become so ingrained in their working vocabulary, both in and out of the studio, that they are unaware of how frequently they use it. "Let's go on" could be the motto of PNB, a phrase used daily and a propulsive leitmotif that recurs throughout the history of the company.

Balanchine said: "I don't have a past. I have a continuous present. The past is part of the present, just as the future is."

Let's go on.

Kent and Francia intent at a rehearsal.

Photo by Kurt Smith.

Following page: The PNB company takes a curtain call

after a performance of Balanchine's Symphony in C *at*

the Kennedy Center in Washington, D.C.

Photo © by Steven Caras.

CLASS I

The pearl light of a Seattle winter day slips through the floor-to-ceiling windows of the studio where dancers sprawl in various angles of stretching or relaxation. They're dressed mostly in stylish grunge: black, white and tattered, here and there a splash of color. Visitors observing through windows in the lobby of Pacific Northwest Ballet's Phelps Center could be forgiven for mistaking the dancers for college students on a break. They are, in fact, accomplished professionals preparing for the challenging 90-minute class they take every working day of their lives. In the language of ballet, it is classe de perfection, *the daily opportunity for dancers to warm up and to perfect their technique.* ❦ *More dancers arrive clutching dance bags and bottled water. Several women tend to their callused feet, applying bandages and tape to their toes and finally swathing them in tissue before plunging them into pink pointe shoes. Two men laugh in friendly competition as they spring into the air as easily as young gazelles and spin once, twice—can it be even more?—before landing softly.* ❦ *Pianist Don Vollema, his blond hair pulled back tight until it cascades in a ponytail, goes to the grand piano in a corner next to the long mirrored wall and warms his fingers: Chopin, show tunes. The dancers arrange portable waist-high iron-pipe barres and take their places. The teacher—Francia on this day—arrives, wearing a gray sweater and slacks and pink shoes with a small heel. She bids the dancers and pianist good morning and says: "First position, pliés. And. . . ." At that signal, the pianist plays adagio. The dancers move as one. Another ballet workday begins.*

St. George and the Dynamite

In the geography of ballet, St. George, Utah, is virtually off the map. Tucked in the southwest corner of Utah, near the Shivwits Indian Reservation and just down the road from the towns of Virgin and Hurricane, St. George is now a retirement boomtown with a population of about 30,000, a warm, sunny spot that boasts of being "the Dixie of Utah." But in 1946, when Harold Stowell, a former all-American basketball player at the University of Idaho, came to St. George to coach basketball and football at Dixie Junior College, the town could count barely 3,000 souls, and soul-counting was important in that Mormon town. Fresh from serving as a major in the U.S. Army, Coach Stowell brought with him his wife, Maxine, and four (soon to be five) children.

The Stowells' second child, a son, gave early indications of being a rascally maverick. Born August 8, 1939, in Rexburg, Idaho, Richard Kent Stowell ("Nobody has ever called me by my first name," he now says, "except car salesmen who look at my driver's license and say, 'How are ya, Dick, let's get you into one of our great new cars, Dick' ") was a cutup who delighted in doing the outrageous to get himself noticed.

"I was always a little bit of a smart aleck," he recalls. "One day when I was about nine, I saw cheerleaders rehearsing in the gym. So I fell down and rolled around and did all sorts of silly stuff. The cheerleaders thought I was so cute they had to have me as a mascot. My mother even got me a mascot's outfit, a sweater and white pants, and trotted me off to games. But when it came to learning all the cheerleader stuff, I couldn't do that, so I was the official mascot only three or four times. But that's how people in St. George looked at me: like a mascot. I was small. My little sister was taller than I was."

In the mid-1940s, St. George's sole window on the world was its movie theatre. It was there that Kent discovered his idol, Fred Astaire. He dreamed of being another Astaire: a tap dancer and a famous movie star who earned "maybe as much as 250 bucks a month!" He may have underestimated the dancer's income but not his superior skill and artistry. He learned later that Balanchine shared his enthusiasm. "The male dancer I like to watch," Balanchine said, "is an American: Fred Astaire. He is the most interesting, the most inventive, the most elegant dancer of our times."

When an itinerant dance teacher came to St. George to conduct a master class, Kent was encouraged to attend. He did and he liked the odds: he was the only boy among about 50 girls. That experience led to his signing up for tap-dance classes with Reynolds Johnson, who was something of a celebrity in St. George because he had been in Hollywood and had danced in a couple of movies.

Opposite: Kent as the Prince in the New York City Ballet's production of Balanchine's Nutcracker. *Photo by Martha Swope.*

Page 11: Vincent Cuny relaxes before class while another dancer stretches. Photo by Kurt Smith.

A Stowell family portrait: Salt Lake City, 1957. Maxine and Harold Stowell are seated. Their children, from left: Bruce, Kent, Barbara, Ben and Laura.

Kent: "In my family we never talked about my dancing. That was really odd. In 1949 or '50 in a little Mormon town, if your young son's a dancer and your father's a coach, there's got to be a lot of talk, but nobody ever said anything to me. I don't remember ever discussing dancing with my father or my siblings. It was like, 'Well, that's just what Kent's doing.' But I think they were thinking, 'What do we *do* with this kid?' My father at least did not discourage me. My mother actively encouraged me. She wanted me to be another Pavlova—that was the only dancer's name she knew. When she took me to see the movie *The Red Shoes* in St. George, we were the only people in the audience. That was my first exposure to ballet."

Young Kent tried his hand at being a musician, first with a hand-me-down trumpet from his mother's half-brother and then with the piano, but he was too much a look-at-me live wire to stay still for long. He more vigorously pursued troublemaking. One day when he was 12, he and a buddy were nosing around a construction site when they found a case of dynamite that workers had failed to conceal completely under a pile of sticks and leaves. Kent and his friend couldn't have been more excited if they'd struck gold and, whooping, they made plans to take the dynamite down to the river and blast it off. But first they stashed it under the floor of the friend's chicken coop so that Kent could race home and brag to his big brother Bruce about his great discovery. Not surprised at Kent's latest caper, Bruce sternly warned him that if he played with dynamite he'd blow his head off and convinced him to return the case. "So we took it back," says Kent. "But I kept the caps and fuses. I'd just roll out 20 feet or so of fuse, put a cap at the end, light the fuse and wait for it to go off. That was fun!" People who know Kent today will have no trouble recognizing the kid in the man.

"Ours was a strict Mormon family, but I didn't know it at the time," says Kent, now a lapsed Mormon. "We had to get down on our knees and pray before every Sunday dinner, and we went to church all the time. Mormonism is not just a church, it's a way of life. There's something going on every day and every evening. My father was hoping we'd all go on missions, but we disappointed him greatly. Only my younger brother Ben went on a mission; he's got three sons and two daughters, just like my father, and he's a coach, too. I haven't ever come to terms with my father, who's now 92. He still calls and says: 'Kent, you've had a great deal of success in your life. You have a good job and a wonderful family. You've done everything except what's important. If you'd just meet God in church, your life would be so much richer and you'd be so much happier.' That's tough to take."

The Stowell family lived in St. George for seven years. In the midst of those years, Coach Stowell turned in his sneakers in order to start an office-supply business. When the business failed, the Stowell family had to make every dollar count, a condition that altered little when the family moved to Salt Lake City, where the elder Stowell found a high school teaching job. Kent continued studying tap dancing at what he calls a "Dolly Dinkle" storefront dance studio and paid for his lessons by hanging around to mop the floors after all the classes were over. After he was encouraged to take ballet classes because they would improve his tap dancing, his mother learned about the University of Utah's dance department, which was run by Willam Christensen, who was part of a noted family of Danish dancers and who staged one of the first *Nutcracker* productions in the United States.

Kent: "I auditioned and was accepted and got a scholarship, because there are never enough boys. My dancing was never discussed at home. My father never said a word, which is amazing because he's an authoritarian type who knows best for all of us, to this day. In Salt Lake City I saw the American Ballet Theatre and the San Francisco Ballet, and there was Erik Bruhn on stage doing things I thought were totally unbelievable. At about 15 or 16, I realized that dancing gave me my identity. I thought: 'This is me. This is my world.' When my English teacher assigned us to write a poem, I wrote a poem about dance, and it was published in the school paper and everyone at school read it. After that, I was always called Twinkletoes. The students looked askance at me. I became sort of antisocial and never did anything in high school activities. Ballet became more and more my safe haven. My parents were struggling with their relationship and with finances. The family was obviously falling apart. (His parents divorced when he was 22.) In St. George, I'd worked as a shoeshine boy in a barber shop and also delivered newspapers, and in Salt Lake City I worked at a Kentucky Fried Chicken store. I didn't worry about missing anything at high school. All the chicks were at ballet class. I had it all worked out."

The Christensen brothers, from left: Willam, Lew and Harold. Photo by George T. Krause. San Francisco Performing Arts Library and Museum photo.

Kent in a San Francisco Ballet studio in 1958.

Kent prided himself on being able to jump high, and he thought if he could do that he didn't need to fuss with actually learning to dance. But learn he did, during three years in the extension division of the University of Utah. After class one day, he met Willam Christensen's brother Lew, the artistic director of the San Francisco Ballet, who had observed class. He told Kent, "If you ever come to San Francisco, you've got a job." "Everybody in ballet was desperate for guys," Kent recalls. "It was almost 'If you're warm in 1957, you're in.' " Soon after his high school graduation, Kent left for San Francisco with a buddy from ballet class, Michael Smuin (who later became artistic director of the San Francisco Ballet).

Kent: "We were determined to let everyone know we were tough, straight guys. We didn't want to be thought of as sissy ballet boys. Mike got an apartment and I lived in a boardinghouse that was near the ballet studios and was full of old men. One old guy had a really good room, but he had to walk through my room to get to it. I thought, 'He's a really old man and if he dies I can get his room.' Well, he did die and I did get his room, but I felt terrible about it for a long time. I was still being a good Mormon, and I still went to church regularly. This impressed my landlady, but I became an oddity in the San Francisco Ballet. As I got to see more of the world, I saw people drinking and smoking, and they were not bad people doing bad things with their lives. That realization shattered my self-confidence. Part of my identity came from being a Mormon. It's hard when you have a strong religious background and then come into the real world.

"But I was doing well in the San Francisco Ballet. I thought I was on top of the world. Recently I found the old W-2 form from that first year. I made $1,300! We danced six *Nutcrackers* and survived, barely, by working for the San Francisco Opera for three months. Leon Kalimos, the manager of the company, helped by getting occasional State Department tours for the company. When we weren't dancing, we could collect unemployment of $24 a week. One time, Leon told the ballet board members that they needed to help Mike and me because we were dead broke. They voted for Leon to buy us each a case of beans!"

Kent was a member of the San Francisco Ballet for five years, moving up through the dancer hierarchy: from member of the corps de ballet to soloist and finally to principal dancer. In the 1960s, being a member of the San Francisco Ballet was a great job for a dancer, but even the nation's oldest established ballet company couldn't assure steady work or reliable income. The State Department tours provided the dancers with employment and a chance to see the world, but most of the dancers still teetered near the poverty line. They could not take advantage of San Francisco's cultural richness because they couldn't even afford transportation to performances, to say nothing of actually buying tickets.

Kent: "In retrospect, I think the San Francisco Ballet at that time was better than people thought but not as good as the company itself said. I was too young to think about whether the work was artistically satisfying. There was a girl in the company I was crazy about. Hormones ran my life. I was trying to grow up, but it took a while. Leon, who was a great salesman and con man, used to tell us that there are only two ballet companies in the world, the New York City Ballet and the San Francisco Ballet. And a lot of naïve dancers, including me, said: 'Well, that's true, and I'm in one of them.' "

To fill layoff time, keep fit and gain more dance experience, Kent and Smuin recruited fellow unemployed dancers and formed a little company called Ballet '61 or '62, or whatever the year was. Kent's first ballet was *The Crucible*, set to a spiritual-based score by Morton Gould; Kent says it was "quite good, for an amateur." His second ballet had music by Bizet and inevitably looked a lot like Balanchine's *Symphony in C*, which is set to Bizet's work of that name.

Kent: "Balanchine was the first influence I thought was reputable. When I first saw his *Concerto Barocco*, I thought, 'This is art! The other stuff is fairy tales!' Balanchine made an art form I could aspire to. I didn't think I ever could aspire to be a prince. It felt, well, silly. Then I did *Serenade* and was fascinated by the way Balanchine manipulated movement to music. This was more an impetus for my interest in ballet than the dancing. I think I was always somewhat of a disappointment as a dancer, though I had talent. They wanted me to be a great dancer, but I didn't have the necessary monomaniacal instinct. I tried hard but I didn't have the kind of self-absorption that you need to be a Nureyev or a Baryshnikov. They're convincing as great dancers because they really believe they *are* great dancers. If you don't deeply believe that, it's not convincing. I was a good dancer, but I was brought up a Mormon. For me, success meant having a family.

Michael Smuin came from Salt Lake City with Kent, and later became artistic director of the San Francisco Ballet. San Francisco Performing Arts Library and Museum photo.

Balanchine and Igor Stravinsky in a New York City Ballet studio. Photo by Martha Swope.

Opposite: Kent applies makeup for his role as the Soldier in The Nutcracker *at the New York City Ballet.*

I wanted to have a home and children and all that domestic stuff. So my focus was not on today but on tomorrow, and the key question was how do I get to tomorrow in pursuit of a financially secure life. I didn't want to be like my father. He has struggled his whole life. All of my middle-class values were important to me, and I don't mean middle-class in a derogatory way. I see it in a very positive sense."

Work with the San Francisco Ballet ultimately didn't seem important to Kent and others in the company. At that time, the New York City Ballet and Balanchine represented the ballet summit. Kent "wanted at least to try to be where it's at." Before the company left for Seattle in the spring of 1962 to perform at the World's Fair, Kent told Lew Christensen that he was leaving the company. It turned out that about half of the dancers were leaving. Although he did not have a job at the New York City Ballet and knew only one person there—Suki Schorer, who had been a member of the San Francisco Ballet— Kent packed all of his possessions and had them shipped to the New York City Ballet. (Kent was never a stranger to chutzpah.) After the Seattle engagement, he boarded a plane with a one-way ticket to New York, "determined to become a member of City Ballet or get out of dance." Two weeks later, he was asked to join the company, and with the New York City Ballet he came back to Seattle to dance at the end of the World's Fair.

Early on, Balanchine asked Kent his age. "Twenty-three," said Kent. "Ha!" Balanchine replied. "When I was twenty-three, I'd already done *Apollo*!" Kent told his new boss that in San Francisco, Leon Kalimos had attempted to compensate the penniless dancers with compliments. "You're all such great dancers," he'd say, "you're all principals." Balanchine listened and then snorted, "In my company, everybody corps!"

CLASS II

Dancers grasp the barre with one hand and, with torso erect, heels touching and toes turned out at 180 degrees from each other, they begin to bend (plier) *slowly down and up, beginning the traditional 90-minute session that suggests both collective ritual and individual meditation. Class opens with* pliés *because they not only are integral to ballet but also are the most efficient way of warming up the large muscles of the leg. "Class is a science as well as an art," Francia says later. Now there is only the sound of the piano and Francia's quietly spoken directions.* ❧ *The dancers move on to* battements tendus, *their straight legs and pointed toes flashing out and in as if they were cutting precise slices of air. Between slices, their feet slap briefly together, touching in parallel and pointing in opposite directions. This turnout is a basic requirement for ballet (and many other dance forms). Coming correctly only from the hip joint and resulting from both anatomy and training, turnout makes it possible for the dancer to move quickly in any direction.* ❧ *The dancers now do* ronds de jambes, *their pointed toes describing a circle first on the floor, then in the air. It becomes clear that proper turnout also gives a dancer's body a more beautiful line: beautiful even when dressed in ragged tights and shaggy sweatshirt.* ❧ *After a few more steps at the barre, Francia calls a break. The dancers stretch, several putting a straight leg over the barre and bending to touch ankle with forehead. Others do apparently comfortable splits on the floor and chat amiably.* ❧ *"I love class," Francia says quietly. "It's the hardest thing I do, but it's the thing I find most rewarding when it works." As it does today.*

Dancing for Daddy

Little Francia Russell was pigeon-toed. Anyone thus configured has small hope of ever becoming a ballet dancer, because ballet requires feet to point out, not in. But spurred on insistently by her father, a failed singer who was determined to have an artist in the family, Francia developed into not just an ordinary ballet dancer but one good enough to be a soloist in the New York City Ballet.

Born in Los Angeles on January 10, 1938, she was three when her family moved to Phoenix, the city where her parents had grown up and where both of her grandfathers had run successful businesses. Her father, Frank Russell, had intended to have an operatic career as a lyric baritone, but bad teaching and singing difficult pieces too soon and too often caused career-ending nodes on his vocal cords. So he found work on radio, writing and presenting scripts about opera, along with playing operatic recordings. When Frank's father died, he moved his family to Phoenix, where he took over his father's photography business. More artist than businessman, he was miserable. After four years in Phoenix, the Russell family moved to Sausalito, across the Golden Gate from San Francisco, a change made possible because Francia's mother, Marion, had inherited "quite a lot of money and property" from her father, a "jolly, generous man" who during many years as *the* Roman Catholic undertaker in Phoenix had accepted payment in the form of property and stocks from those unable to pay for funerals in cash.

Francia recalls: "My sister Marilyn was Daddy's great hope. Even very young she had a beautiful voice, but she refused to study music. Mullen—she always had nicknames; I wanted one but never had any that stuck—was an outgoing kid, very pretty, loved by everybody, and she always hugged everybody. I was shy and awkward and quiet and always wanted to go read a book. I had big bony knees and elbows and ears sticking out. I was not God's gift. Mullen and I often got all dressed up and were taken to performances at the Opera House in San Francisco. One night after we saw Danilova dance, Mullen decided she wanted to study ballet. Daddy was thrilled. He arranged for lessons and made me go along, too. I was such a klutz. I had bloody knees all the time because I was very pigeon-toed and was always falling down. I was a tomboy, loved to climb trees. But I was always messing up. I think Daddy believed that ballet lessons would be good for me. So we were taken to the San Francisco Ballet School. Mullen quit after six months. She said it was too hard, she hated it, and she wouldn't go anymore. I didn't like the lessons at all, but Harold Christensen, the director of the school, told Daddy I had a good body for ballet and was very talented.

"So I started dancing when I was seven. Daddy watched every class, sitting upright on a bench, so severe and always correcting me. I cried all the time. Daddy knew nothing

Opposite: Francia in the New York City Ballet's production of Swan Lake. *Photo by Fred Fehl.*

Page 21: Leah Belliston (left) and Lisa Apple schmooze before class. Photo by Kurt Smith.

about ballet, but he would roll back the rug in our living room, bring out the barre and make me practice. I remember one time when my grandmother came to visit, the three of us went to my teacher's house. They stood me in the center of the room, turned on some music, and I was supposed to come up with a dance. Daddy and Grandmother sat and waited, but I couldn't move, I couldn't dance. I just stood there and bawled. Daddy wasn't cruel or anything like that, but he had wanted so much to be an internationally famous opera star that he felt the greatest gift he could give his daughters was to have them become artists. I'm sure he was convinced that he was doing something good for me. And he did, actually."

Marion Russell, whose inherited money was buoying the family, usually deferred to her husband, but after he had a "nervous breakdown" in 1948, she took the initiative to sell the house in Sausalito and move the family to Europe. Frank had always wanted to go to Europe, and his wife thought the move "might save him," a hope that happily turned into reality. Their first stop was Paris, where Frank was thrilled to communicate with the Grand Duke Andrei and arrange for his daughter to have private lessons with the legendary Mme. Kschessinksa. "By that time, she was 90-something," says Francia. "The lessons were worthless."

When a doctor said that Marilyn needed to live in a sunny climate, the Russells moved to Nice, where they stayed for two years. Again networking, Frank contacted a member of the Ballet Russe de Monte Carlo whom he had known in San Francisco. So that's where Francia studied. "I was ten and I was taking class with the company," she says. "It was silly and incredibly intimidating. But they were very nice to me, because I was a little kid."

In Nice, Frank started work on a book about Henrietta Sontag, a 19th-century German soprano who had already been the subject of a biography by no less a writer than Théophile Gautier. Frank decided he needed to do research at the British Museum, so the family moved to London. Now 12, Francia auditioned for the Royal Ballet School and was turned down. Because her father was 6'1" and she was the older daughter, she was told that she would grow too tall to be a ballet dancer. Besides, the school said, her toes were too long, she should never put on toe shoes, she should dance barefoot like Isadora Duncan! "When I received my first soloist contract from the New York City Ballet," says Francia, "I wanted to send it to those people at the Royal Ballet. If there had been Xerox machines then, I would have."

Being rebuffed by the Royal Ballet School actually turned out to be to her advantage, because she ended up studying with Vera Volkova, another legendary Russian teacher but one who exceeded all expectations. Volkova was, according to Francia, "the great teacher in my life." In her studio, Francia met ballet's *crème de la crème*; she took class with members of visiting companies from all over the world, and she was able to observe Volkova's private coaching sessions with such stars as Margot Fonteyn and David Blair. She had yet another memorable teacher in London: a tutor who introduced her to English literature, art and history and then took her to the very places where all of it had been created. Francia wrote essays about what she'd seen, read or heard. "It was the most fun learning I've ever had," she says. "All of us loved London and would have stayed there forever, but we couldn't get the proper papers so we had to go back to the States."

The Russells sailed for San Francisco via the Panama Canal, and every day during the six-week trip Francia worked at the barre on deck, with her father coaching her. Having completed his book and finding himself back in the States with no job, Frank decided to develop the property his wife had inherited. At the time it was taken as payment for funerals, the property had small value, but it was located at the foot of Camelback Mountain: precisely the area later developed for upscale resorts and homes for Phoenix's high-rollers. In just two years, Frank lost everything and ended up owing money. But enough of the inheritance remained to make possible another move: to New York City.

Francia: "Camelback kept my father awake nights for the rest of his life. But there must have been money somewhere, because we saw everything in New York. At 14, I was crazy about the American Ballet Theatre and Alonso and Youskevitch and Lupé Serrano and Erik Bruhn. I'd quit dancing when we arrived in New York and gone to a Catholic convent school, but after three months I started studying dance again with Benjamin Harkarvy, who was a very strong positive influence. I studied with lots of teachers in lots of places, wherever someone told my father they'd make me a star, but I never was with students my own age in a disciplined, structured curriculum. Boy, do I appreciate now what that means for the kids in PNB's school!"

Francia's parents: Frank and Marion Russell.

Opposite: Francia (foreground) with Balanchine and Stravinsky at a rehearsal for the premiere of Agon *by the* New York City Ballet. Photo by Martha Swope.

With the desperation that only teenagers can feel, Francia wanted to become a member of American Ballet Theatre, but that company's ruling eminence, Lucia Chase, said no: too tall (at 5'6") and not pretty enough. But as had happened with the Royal Ballet, rejection proved beneficial. Francia was accepted at the School of American Ballet, which Lincoln Kirstein had started for Balanchine in the 1930s.

Francia: "The word was that if you were at SAB, Mr. B. might come in at any time, and if he liked you, he'd take you into the company [the New York City Ballet]. I'd been at SAB only three weeks when the school administrator told me that Balanchine had seen me and liked me, and I should call the company manager about a contract. I called and she said she'd never heard of me; there was no contract. She said the company was on layoff for three more weeks, so I waited and waited, didn't eat and didn't sleep, just waited. Finally a couple of girls didn't come back after the layoff, and I was hired. I was 18. Back then the company was small, about 40. [It now has about 90 dancers.] I learned so many ballets so fast that I don't even know how it was possible. I was in *everything*. Four girls, eight girls, 24 girls, solos and then principal roles—I was doing it all. I was so tired I didn't know who I was anymore. But I started getting wonderful roles, and then I got my soloist contract."

Francia was living with her family on Riverside Drive, near Columbia University. Her father's book about Mme. Sontag had been published, but the only returns he had from his continuing daily writing were rejection slips. He tried a number of businesses, all unsuccessful. Finally he became head of the front desk at the Whitney Museum. Meanwhile, Marion took various jobs, including positions at the Bank Street School and as a receptionist for an ophthalmologist, eventually becoming an assistant in eye operations. Frank continued at the Whitney until he retired at 65. "He was always embarrassed about his lack of career and accomplishments," says Francia. "Finally he could say he was a retired writer and he had worked at the Whitney. He was a happy man. When he was 69, they discovered inoperable stomach cancer."

Francia: "The New York City Ballet *was* Balanchine. There was enormous excitement in working for him and in feeling that I understood what he wanted. He choreographed on me a lot because I understood it quickly. He was such an interesting man. And of course, I loved dancing his ballets. They were physically, intellectually, spiritually challenging and satisfying. It was such an exciting time at City Ballet. Stravinsky was around, and there was the feeling that this was the center of the universe. I was lucky to be working with Balanchine during his most creative years. I loved his classes. After one of those you felt you'd done everything of which your mind and your body were capable.

On layoff, he taught three-hour classes. I used to go downtown and take classes with Bob Joffrey so I'd be warmed up for Mr. B.'s classes. He expected perfect turnout to begin with, and I wanted to be ready. He was a gentleman, but he could be cruel. His lack of interest in someone was a death blow for that person. He wanted us to be like nuns, devoted to ballet. We wanted to please him too much and ourselves not enough. We sure did want to please him. Never mind about the audience. We were dancing for him."

But remember the pigeon-toed little girl? The stress of many years of forcing turnout from hips that weren't made for ballet finally caught up with Francia. Although she had developed muscles to achieve turnout, that created excess torque on her knees, and finally she tore knee cartilage. The pain was extreme and insistent, but she danced through it. For a while. After five years with the New York City Ballet, she quit dancing. She was only 23.

Francia: "It was not just the pain that made me quit. I was tired out, exhausted from all the pressure that had been on me from the time I was seven. Besides, I had an insatiable curiosity about the world outside ballet, and when I was dancing I couldn't begin to satisfy that curiosity. I had very little real outside life."

She studied at NYU, Columbia and the New School for Social Research and got a job managing an art gallery at 65th and Madison. She returned to the School of American Ballet, this time as a teacher. At SAB she heard that a handsome new dancer from San Francisco had joined City Ballet and was going to be at a party thrown by the company's wardrobe master. Francia decided she'd go, too.

And that's how the cosmopolitan lass from San Francisco/Paris/Nice/London and New York met the rascally lad from St. George, Utah.

Opposite: Francia and Francisco Moncion in the New York City Ballet's production of Firebird. Photo by Fred Fehl.

29

CLASS III

The dancers carry the portable barres to the side of the studio, then arrange themselves in lines and begin "center" work. Again they start with battements tendus *but with no barre to hold to steady their balance. Straight legs and pointed toes flash out and in: quick movements that stretch and smooth out leg muscles. Such rapid, darting movements prevent leg muscles from bulking up and thus are crucial for female dancers, who strive to project a long pure line; the prominent leg muscles of the men, which they need for lifting and leaping, are developed through jumping and weight training.* ❦ *The dancers complete the* tendus. *As if talking to herself, Francia quietly indicates the next exercise, often illustrating her words with rapid movements of her hands and feet. The instructions are so minimal—and some of the dancers are apparently paying so little attention—that it seems a small miracle when the music starts and all the dancers move precisely together.* ❦ *Although ballet's beginnings were in Italy in the 15th century, its language is French, the word* ballet *being the French adaptation of the Italian* balletto, *meaning "little dance." All ballet steps have French names, many dating to 1700 when French ballet master Raoul Feuillet codified them in his book,* Choréographie. *Over the years, steps were added by other French ballet masters, most notably Jean Georges Noverre in the mid-18th century. Because the language of ballet is universal, dancers can take class wherever it is taught.* ❦ *Francia now begins to put steps together into combinations, again giving only slight verbal and movement indications to the dancers, who obviously have learned to "read" her coded instructions. In their graceful, often astonishing movements, the dancers find freedom within constraint and create beauty out of what could be merely repetitious movement.*

"Not as Bad as I Expected"

Francia now had two men pursuing her, Kent and Balanchine. The latter was eager to persuade her to come back to his company. When he'd spot her at a performance, he'd come up and, in his thick Russian accent, hold out enticements to her to dance again: "Wouldn't you like to go with us on tour to Russia, dear?" She said no, convinced that she was right in quitting the company. But she wasn't always negative with Kent, with whom she was having a relationship "with many ons and offs."

Teaching at the School of American Ballet was for Francia an eye-opener that also gave her invaluable experience. Balanchine often observed her as she taught class, and afterward he'd go over with her all the details of the class—and cite everything he found wrong. That obviously was intimidating, but it was also illuminating. In those after-class sessions, "Mr. B. really taught me what class is all about," Francia says. But for all the artistic rewards of teaching at SAB, she quit after a year because she wasn't making enough money to support herself. Then, indulging in a little giddy fun after decades of artistic dedication, she left New York to dance in summer-stock musicals. When she came back to the city, she got a job as an editorial assistant at *Publishers Weekly*; after about six months there, she had a conversation with Barbara Horgan, then Balanchine's personal assistant and later the executrix of the Balanchine Trust.

Francia: "Barbara said the company was going to Washington, D.C., to do a benefit for Lyndon Johnson and they needed a girl for *Stars and Stripes* and would I go. Then she said, 'If you've ever thought of being a ballet mistress, I'd recommend that you talk with Mr. Balanchine on this trip.' He'd obviously said something to her, but he wasn't going to ask me again. I thought, well, Kent's at City Ballet, and I was gradually getting to the point where ballet didn't look as awful to me. Besides, Mr. B. had already sent me to Montreal to stage his *Allegro Brillante*, and he'd taken me by the hand and taught me how to teach. So one day in Washington when Mr. B. was sitting alone in the house, I went out and asked if he'd consider me for a position as ballet mistress. He said only one word: 'Yes.' That was that: I was back in the company."

A ballet mistress and ballet master are the principal dance assistants to a company's artistic director, a position Balanchine occupied but a title he never used, affecting humility by calling himself simply ballet master. Ballet mistresses/masters have multiple major responsibilities: knowing and teaching the company's repertoire, overseeing rehearsals and performances, and teaching class. A few years ago, a caller to PNB in Seattle, apparently checking on something she'd read in a PNB program, asked for clarification of what work Francia had done with the five-times-married Balanchine. "She was his

Opposite: Kent and Suzanne Farrell in the New York City Ballet's production of Balanchine's Liebeslieder Waltzer. *Photo by Martha Swope.*

Page 31: Francia teaching class at PNB. Photo by Kurt Smith.

ballet mistress," said the PNB receptionist. "Oh," replied the caller, "I'd heard he had many of *those*, too."

Francia: "Mr. B. kept after me to dance. I took class every day, and he'd come up and ask if I didn't want this or that wonderful role. I said no. Knowing what my favorite ballet was, he'd ask, 'Wouldn't you like to do *Apollo*, dear?' I always said no. But I did dance in the corps when someone was injured. I really had to know *everything*."

Francia continued to see Kent, who was steadily getting more and better roles at City Ballet. John Cranko, a South African choreographer who headed the highly regarded Stuttgart Ballet, asked Francia to found and direct the school for his company. She declined the offer and stayed in New York, because at the time her relationship with Kent was more on than off. The more the two saw of each other, the more they realized that they shared not only opinions about ballet but also deeply felt ideas about marriage, family and home. On November 19, 1965, at the Unitarian Church at 56th and Broadway, Kent and Francia were married.

Francia: "I very much wanted to marry. I really wanted to have children. I'd wanted to have children since I was two, I think. I treated my sister like my own baby, and I was only a year and 18 days older. My father didn't want me to have children. Neither did Mr. B." (He once said to another dancer: "Every woman can become a mother, but not every woman can become a ballerina.")

Kent: "Balanchine didn't like our being married. It was hard on Francia because he liked to torture her."

Francia: "He would leave Kent out of casting and wait to see if I said anything. Whatever I did was wrong. He was very difficult."

Kent: "Others in City Ballet were married, but we were the only married couple in the company. For whatever reason, Balanchine made us suffer for being married. I'm sure that drove us more together than apart. When we had our first child, Balanchine

Maria Tallchief and Kent.

Kent as Romeo in John Cranko's Romeo and Juliet, *performing in Munich in 1972.*

came over to our apartment on West 69th near Lincoln Center, took a look at little Christopher and said, 'Not as bad as I expected.' "

Although Kent had been promoted to soloist and was dancing prized roles, doubts about his and his family's future nagged him. During his sixth year with City Ballet, questions intensified: "I kept wondering where dancing was going to take me and how I should get out of it. I was 28 and that's when you start thinking about your future without dance. Besides, it was a very uncomfortable time at City Ballet because Suzanne Farrell, the dancer Balanchine was in love with, dominated the company, and he didn't think about much else."

Francia: "Shortly after Kent quit, Suzanne got married and left. Balanchine really fell apart. He went away for a long time. For months he was in Europe."

Kent: "That was good for Francia because when Balanchine was gone, she virtually ran the company. There wasn't anyone else to do it."

After Kent made the difficult decision and stopped dancing, he worked for a year for Francia's brother-in-law in Manhattan's garment district, at a job he describes as "an experience from Dickens." The idea of college teaching appealed to his instinct for security, so he sent letters to many universities. The most positive response came from the University of Indiana, and when he and Francia went to Bloomington for an interview, the dean was enthusiastic about their ideas, specifically their proposal to start a high school for the performing arts because by the time students enroll in college, it's too late for them to start ballet. They returned to New York, packed up and moved to Bloomington.

Kent: "It was hard to leave Balanchine and New York. We continued to have second thoughts about it for many years. I felt dreadfully guilty of having taken Francia away from a very successful career. She went along with my decisions, even when I thought I was an idiot half the time. I think part of growing up is making mistakes and figuring out how to overcome them; certainly all our concerns and anxieties about coming to Seattle turned out to be productive and motivating. When we arrived in Bloomington, the dean acted as if he'd never heard of any of our ideas. They weren't written into my contract. Later he told me, 'You know, Kent, you've got a lot to learn about negotiations.' We'd been there less than two weeks when Francia told me not to bother unpacking the books, because we couldn't survive there more than a single academic year. That's when we decided to go to Europe."

After another flurry of letter-writing, Kent received an offer to be principal dancer and choreographer of the Bavarian State Opera Ballet in Munich. Francia put aside her aversion to Germany, where she had traveled to stage Balanchine ballets, and agreed to move there—but for only one year. That one year stretched into seven, three in Munich and four in Frankfurt. Francia had no job with the ballet company in Munich, and at Balanchine's request she staged his ballets throughout Europe.

Kent: "Our second son, Darren, was born while we were in Munich. Francia was very happy then, and I don't think she cared where we were. The situation was great for me. I was dancing and getting a chance to choreograph, and that's not something you learn other than by on-the-job training. When we moved to Frankfurt, I stopped dancing and was ballet master and choreographer of the Frankfurt Ballet for two years. We had another son, Ethan [their third and last child], and I think Francia was happy in our nice house in the country. During our last two years in Germany, Francia and I were artistic directors of the Frankfurt Ballet. It was a good company, and we did some good work there, including a new production of *Swan Lake*. We had some wonderful times in Germany. Many parts of the country are stunningly beautiful, and the Germans themselves are so neat and fastidious. I enjoyed seeing our kids in lederhosen and laughing. I watched them happily learn German faster than I possibly could. But there were difficulties. In that homogenous society, we were foreigners. The key reason we left Germany was our desire to go home."

Francia: "We wanted the boys to grow up in their own country."

Kent with son Christopher at Lincoln Center in New York City.

CLASS IV

As class progresses, the dancers' movements become bigger, broader, more dynamic. Hollow popping sounds fill the studio as the tips of the women's toe shoes strike the floor almost simultaneously, again and again. The gray floor, coated with rosin from the dancers' shoes, is etched with countless streaks and smudges left by thousands of shoes over hundreds of weeks. ❦ *Almost all of the women have their hair pulled back tight and gathered into a bun, a practical style for class and rehearsal. "Bunhead" is dancers' slang for a dancer who eats right, sleeps right, lives right, exercises right, cares carefully for her shoes and clothes, and is, in Marine parlance, gung ho.* ❦ *The men now soaring across the studio in controlled leaps are clearly more athletic than a platoon of Marines—or a smash of football players, a dunk of basketball players. They achieve amazing elevation with what seems the slightest of effort, and they land softly, quietly. The indentation of the "sprung" floor is apparent as they land.* ❦ *The floor that cushions the landings, and thus is crucial in preventing injuries, is made of fir stringers that measure 1 by 3 inches and are arranged in a basket-weave configuration in three layers with rubber cushions between layers; that then is topped with sheets of white pine tongue-and-groove plywood and covered with a thin, tough vinyl surface. For performances in the Opera House and on tour, the company uses a portable stage assembled from 4-by-8-foot sections of similar construction. It takes 112 sections for the Opera House stage; each section costs $300; PNB owns more than 200 sections. The dancers wouldn't be without the portable stage; it accompanied them in 1996 to Washington, D.C., and New York.* ❦ *The women land softly on the cushioned floor after soaring in* grands jetés, *which are like flying splits three feet off the ground. Not for the first time, one wonders:* How do they do that?

Sputtering in Seattle

An ocean and a continent away from Germany, Seattle was struggling to get a new dance company on its feet. Many leading American dancers and choreographers got their start in Seattle, but even the most charitable description of the city's dance scene from the mid-1960s to the mid-1970s would likely include the phrase "a mess." The balkanization of the Seattle dance community made politics in the Balkans look orderly.

Seattle enriched American dance by exporting Merce Cunningham, Robert Joffrey, Gerald Arpino and Karel Shook and later nurtured Trisha Brown, Mark Morris and Val Caniparoli. A list of top dancers from Seattle—Francesca Corkle, William Whitener, Dana Shapiro, Ann Reinking, William Weslow—could go on and on, as could a list of good dance teachers in the area—Mary Ann Wells, Karen Irvin, Ruthanna Boris, Marion and Illaria Ladre, Dorothy Fisher, Martha Nishitani, Perry Brunson. Imports to Seattle included two former New York City Ballet principal dancers, Janet Reed and Melissa Hayden, who were employed, successively, to build a fire under a new professional ballet company in Seattle, but the homegrown product sputtered on the launching pad, creating more sparks than lift.

PNB evolved out of a primordial alphabet soup that included PNBA, PND and PNDB. Pacific Northwest Ballet Association was founded in 1966 to raise the money necessary to qualify for a grant from the National Endowment for the Arts that would bring the City Center Joffrey Ballet to the Pacific Northwest for a summer residency and short performance season. Funds secured, Seattle native Robert Joffrey brought his company from New York in the summer of 1967 for five performances at the Seattle Opera House and a residency at Pacific Lutheran University in the Tacoma area. The same arrangement was repeated in the summer of 1968. In response to complaints that Joffrey was siphoning off support money that could be better used by local dance groups, PNBA declared its intention to provide "in the near future a professional regional company based in the Northwest." Although PNBA increasingly had difficulty in raising money, it brought the Joffrey company back in the summers of 1969 and 1970.

According to a valuable chronology prepared by Sheila C. Dietrich, in August 1970 Dr. Hans Lehmann, PNBA's president, noted that there was uncertainty about continued NEA support and a slackening of interest in the Joffrey company. In 1971, PNBA dropped its association with the Joffrey company and voted to support the much smaller and much less expensive First Chamber Dance Company, headed by Charles Bennett, a former New York City Ballet dancer. But money problems snowballed for PNBA. In October 1972, Bennett accused PNBA of causing the collapse of his company by default-

Opposite: 1975 Pacific Northwest Dance performance. PNB photo.

Page 39: PNB principal dancer Manard Stewart leaps high in class. Photo by Kurt Smith.

Glynn Ross, general director of Seattle Opera.

Seattle Opera photo.

ing on its payments, and although the amount of the debt was disputed, Don Franklin, then PNBA's president, admitted that PNBA owed money to Bennett's company. Under fire from the press, from its creditors and from virtually all sectors of the Seattle dance community, PNBA ducked and ran for cover.

Glynn Ross, the flamboyant general director of the Seattle Opera, came to the rescue by proposing that PNBA come "under the umbrella" of Seattle Opera. PNBA would "remain dormant" until its creditors were satisfied and its contractual arrangements settled and then would either dissolve or merge with a newly created organization called Pacific Northwest Dance. The PNBA board voted unanimously to accept Ross's offer, and on November 20, 1972, PND filed articles of incorporation, with Ross named as general director, Harold Heath as president, and a board consisting of 16 members from the Opera board and 15 members from the PNBA board.

The ambitions of the new PND can be inferred from an application it made for a charitable donation permit. The application stated that receipts from a two-month fund drive in early 1973 would be used "to fund an artistic director, a Northwest-based dance company and other nonprofit dance groups." All of that from a fund drive whose goal was a mere $32,000!

Ross was a crackerjack promoter of Seattle Opera. A short, wiry, endlessly articulate man who had earned his crooked nose as a champion boxer in his boyhood Nebraska, Ross caught Seattle's attention with such gimmicks as bumper stickers saying "Get Ahead with *Salome* at Seattle Opera." He had trained to be a Shakespearean actor, but after serving in the U.S. Army in Italy in World War II, he stayed on in Naples after the war and became an opera director. His concept of a dance company, therefore, was based on the European model: dance as opera's subordinate partner, a company used to provide dances for opera productions and only occasionally to present full dance programs on the opera company's night off.

In the summer of 1973, the Joffrey company returned to Seattle, this time sponsored by PND. Its performances were so successful that at its first annual meeting in August, PND reported a surplus of $26,958, even though its fund drive was $13,000 short of its $40,000 goal. At that meeting, PND's board took an action that turned out to be crucial to the company's future success: it elected Sheffield Phelps, an influential Seattle businessman and former president of Seattle Opera, as its president. A few weeks later, Ross announced his plan for "establishing a major dance company," and Leon Kalimos, former executive director of the San Francisco Ballet (the same man who once got cases of beans for Kent Stowell and Michael Smuin), was hired to manage the new company.

Kalimos wrote Kent in Germany and encouraged him to think about coming to Seattle to be artistic director of the new company; several letters were exchanged before Kent sent his regrets after Kalimos informed him that PND couldn't afford to fly him to Seattle for discussions.

Janet Reed, a former principal dancer of the New York City Ballet, came to Seattle to establish and direct PND's school. She chose 42 young dancers for scholarships in summer classes that were held in the only available space: an old municipal bathhouse the city had converted into a dance studio. Lew Christensen, artistic director of the San Francisco Ballet, came north to initiate a professional development program for dancers. Scholarship dancers appeared in Seattle Opera's production of *Aida* at Expo '74 in Spokane and in the Opera's Seattle season opener, *Mefistofele*; these were the first appearances of dancers under the PND aegis.

Reed became PND's ballet mistress in July 1974, and Phelps began scouring Seattle for a suitable home for the new company and its school. He finally came upon the Home of the Good Shepherd in the Wallingford neighborhood of north-central Seattle. The imposing stone structure was built in 1906 to house "wayward girls," a phrase which in those days meant needy young women who were out on their own; they found both home and employment at the Home of the Good Shepherd, which took in laundry from the railroads. By 1974, there were virtually no railroads, let alone railroad laundry, and the big building was occupied only by a few nuns. PND opened two studios there in November 1974 and, with tiny administrative offices and the addition of two more studios, the building served as the company's home for more than nine years.

The good news at PND's annual meeting in November 1974 was of financial stability, thanks in part to hot-ticket business by the Joffrey company earlier that year. The bad news was that the press almost unanimously dismissed "the dance wing of Seattle Opera," preferring instead to award its laurels and support to the First Chamber Dance

Lew Christensen (left) and Leon Kalimos on the San Francisco Ballet set for Christensen's Nutcracker. San Francisco Performing Arts Library and Museum photo.

Company, which was back in business in Seattle. Kalimos continued his correspondence with Kent in Frankfurt, and in one letter he enclosed a brochure that listed Kent as a faculty member at PND's summer school. (This was news to Kent, who took no part in the school. Later he wrote Kalimos, deftly slicing the wry: "I heard I was in Seattle in the summer. How did I like it?") Janet Reed soldiered on with the school, whose enrollment grew to 230, but PND lost money on the Joffrey company because an enterprising theatre manager in Spokane scheduled the Panovs, an illustrious Russian dancing couple, with the San Francisco Ballet only four days after the Joffrey visit to Spokane.

In December 1975, PND presented its first *Nutcracker*, with choreography by Lew Christensen, guest soloists Cynthia Gregory and Ivan Nagy, and four dancers on PND contracts; the rest of the dancers were advanced students from the school. Six performances were announced and sold out; two performances were added, and they also sold out quickly.

In March 1976, the City of Seattle bought the Home of the Good Shepherd, changing its name to the Good Shepherd Center and putting the Historic Seattle Preservation and Development Authority in charge of its operation, with PND as the principal occupant. The following May, PND again presented the Joffrey company, precipitating a disagreeable dispute over the divvying up of revenues. Another blow came in July when Janet Reed chose not to renew her contract as ballet mistress and director of the school.

Still a resident of Seattle, Reed, never known for mincing words, recently commented on leaving PNB: "I was suffering burnout. I was working too hard with much too much to handle. And it didn't seem to be going anywhere. I wasn't getting the proper support. There was every reason in the world not to stay."

Within weeks PND hired another famous dancer, Melissa Hayden, to be ballet mistress, and her husband, Donald Coleman, was named director of the school. At PND's 1976 annual meeting, the budget figures were impressive: revenue for fiscal 1976 was $477,055 (up from $217,799 in FY 1975); expenses were $470,707 (up from $248,558). The ink was black! There was more good news when four season-preview performances, prepared by Todd Bolender, nearly sold out and excited positive word of mouth. Ten performances of a repeat of Christensen's *Nutcracker* sold out six weeks ahead of schedule; an added performance sold out in three hours.

But there was bad news as well. Kalimos was injured in an auto accident that sent him into surgery and a long recuperation. He had been a vigorous promoter with big ideas and energetic salesmanship, even if he occasionally cut dubious corners; he had hustled up a lot of business for PND and helped it achieve nearly 80 percent of its budget in

To Denise—
Wishing you all
the best always,
love,
Janet

Opposite: Vivian Little is held high in PND's debut,

in the Seattle Opera's production of Aida.

Photo by Des Gates & Associates.

earned income over a three-year period. But by the time of his accident it was clear to everyone associated with PND that Hayden and Kalimos had temperaments that were, to be charitable, not congenial. And it wasn't only each other that Kalimos and Hayden rubbed the wrong way.

Phelps recalls having dinner with Hayden in early spring 1977: "I told Melissa that she had to stop teaching class and rehearsing with a cigarette always hanging out of her month, and that, while her gutter language might be okay for New York, it was unacceptable in Seattle. I told her she was being a very poor role model for the young students in our school. She looked at me and said, 'All right, Shef, then I quit.' And I said: 'Melissa, I accept your resignation.' When board members found out what had happened, they were up in arms and said I couldn't do that without approval of the board. I told them that Melissa had quit and that, as president, I had accepted her resignation, and if that wasn't good enough for them, they'd better get a new president." Some years later, Phelps was asked why he stuck with the ballet company through thick and thin—mostly thin. "I don't like to lose," he said.

The press, which had been almost gleefully covering the not-so-secret differences within PND, rallied around Hayden and excoriated PND officials, with "philistines" being among the lesser charges. With Hayden scheduled to leave after her new production of *Coppélia* in May, Kalimos returned from his sickbed, received a vote of confidence from the board, and went to see Kent and Francia in Frankfurt. This time PND agreed to pop for Kent's airfare. After discussions in Seattle about PND's present status and its plans for the future, Kent returned to Frankfurt and told Francia they could pack the books. On May 12, 1977, the PND board named Kent artistic director and Francia associate artistic director and director of the school.

Melissa Hayden, PND's ballet mistress (right), with Mrs. H. Dewayne Kreager, chair of the PND Ballet League.

Seattle Times photo by Larry Dion.

CLASS V

The blue-skied warmth of a spring day, so brilliant that it compensates for the many gray days and makes local boosterism seem understated, floods into Studio C. It's a day to be outdoors. But for the PNB company, it's 10 o'clock, time for class. ❧ *Kent is teaching the women today, and although class begins with the usual* pliés *and* battements tendus, *it's soon clear that his teaching style differs markedly from Francia's. While Francia artfully works with the dancers to perfect their technique, Kent is more spontaneous and experimental. Francia seeks to increase the dancers' sense of security in their technique. Kent wants to explore how far they can go with their technique, both to test the dancers' versatility and to exercise his choreographic creativity.* ❧ *Kent claps sharply in time with the music, making occasional corrections, clearly insistent on quick, accurate movement. As class proceeds, the dancers pass through warming up to being hot. Tattered sweaters and sweatshirts are shed and tossed aside, often revealing more tattered garb underneath. While the pianist frolics through a bouncy "Nice Work If You Can Get It," the dancers spin quickly, the sound of squeaking toe shoes contrasting with the visual fluidity of their pirouettes.* ❧ *Kent asks for a combination of steps that begins with eight counts of moving on pointe. His tippy-toe approximation makes the dancers laugh. Kent returns the good humor and continues demonstrating the combination he has confected. The dancers, still smiling, shrug their shoulders; several throw up their hands. Kent urges them at least to try. Four dancers do try, and break out in giggles. The pianist plays "Let's Call the Whole Thing Off." Kent revises the combination, and now the dancers virtually bubble through the steps.* ❧ *Ninety minutes pass. Kent applauds and thanks the dancers. Their customary class-ending applause is longer than usual.*

"We Have to Be the Best"

Kent, Francia and their three sons arrived in Seattle late in July 1977. They were met at the airport by the PND School secretary, who took them to a motel on Aurora Avenue, a neon-lit small-business arterial that is less than the best introduction to Seattle. Flowers from PND were waiting at the motel, but the repatriated expats faced a long list of disheartening developments:

※ Sheffield Phelps and Jerome Sanford, the two men who had convinced Kent of PND's support for his ideas, were unavailable. Phelps, who had become PND chairman, was out of town; Sanford, a key PND board member, was having open-heart surgery.

※ Leon Kalimos, who had recruited Kent and Francia, was ineffective not only because of lingering effects of his auto accident and surgery but also because of increased friction between him and PND leaders.

※ The Seattle media, which had a history of being skeptical about PND, had turned openly hostile when their favorite, Melissa Hayden, left town. Writers questioned the competence of Kent and Francia: "Who are you two to build a successful ballet company if someone as famous as Melissa Hayden couldn't do it?" A reporter for a Seattle daily even accused them of being frauds, of lying about their credentials.

※ The few professional dancers Hayden had brought to Seattle had dispersed elsewhere when she departed; the PND company was essentially a blank slate.

※ PND's school lacked a coherent structure and curriculum and was woefully short of experienced teachers.

※ Francia was horrified when she attended an opera performance at the Seattle Opera House. She despaired of building a ballet company in the cavernous expanse of the 3,000-seat theatre. She cried throughout the performance.

Then the Let's-Go-On Syndrome kicked in. Kent and Francia went to work, with the impossible imperative of doing everything at once. In the atmosphere of media animosity and with the PND board smarting over losing its first two artistic leaders, Kent and Francia quickly had to prove their competence and their ability to deal with difficult situations. They had to convince PND board members, who understandably were eager for at least some small token of success, that building a ballet company is a long, slow process. Moreover, they had to audition dancers and build a company from scratch.

Kent: "We didn't have any specific timeline. We just trudged along, doing our work. From the beginning, our relations with the board have been unusual. We've been to every board meeting since we've been here, and we've stayed as long as board members needed explanations or answers."

Opposite: Kent demonstrates a step during rehearsal at the Good Shepherd Center. Photo by David Melody.

Page 49: Kent and Francia in a morning class at the Good Shepherd Center. Photo by Kurt Smith.

Francia staging Balanchine's La Valse *for the Stuttgart Ballet.*

To increase communication, Kent met with PND president David B. Winder and other key board members every Tuesday morning. They gathered at a McDonald's and, over Egg McMuffins, discussed PND business. After the company nibbled at success, the Tuesday morning meetings were upgraded—to Denny's.

Francia brought order to the school, establishing five levels for students of different ages and abilities (the school now has ten levels) and crafting a syllabus, which set guidelines for the type and progression of steps taught at each level. The new ordering of levels upset the students (and their parents), who had been accustomed to taking whatever class they liked.

Francia and Kent taught classes every day, usually all day long, and somehow squeezed in meetings and rehearsals as well. After long days they went home to their domestic routine: Francia helped the boys with their baths and homework while Kent, like Balanchine a gourmet cook, prepared dinner.

At state-funded theatres in Germany, Kent and Francia hadn't had to deal with a board, worry about fund-raising or work to educate a community (and a board) about ballet. Their learning curve in Seattle was nearly vertical, and they worked hard at it, all the while doing the square-one job of teaching students and nurturing a company. Their almost palpable dedication did not go unnoticed.

"I don't think they understood how big a challenge they'd taken on," Phelps said recently. "But they came here and, bless them, slowly but surely we worked our way through one problem after another. It was Kent and Francia and their dedication that started making what exists today: an excellent ballet company that is extraordinary because those who are a part of it feel they are truly a part of a family. Kent and Francia provide fairness and caring and the sense of family."

Before the end of 1977, the board took a number of important actions: it terminated its sponsorship of the Joffrey company, approved the signing of contracts with 18 dancers, and did not renew Kalimos's contract. In December, the renewal of Lew Christensen's *Nutcracker* attracted a sellout crowd for 14 performances.

Francia: "We had to clamp down hard on the students—and their parents. We told them, 'If your child is going to be in *Nutcracker*, they have to be here for every rehearsal. If they can't, then they can't be in *Nutcracker*.' We had to instill a professional attitude."

A key imperative was to increase public visibility of the company and begin to convince everyone (including a few trustees) that the homegrown ballet company could present first-rate performances without being bolstered by imported (and expensive) stars. For mixed-repertoire performances in February and April 1978, Kent choreographed four new ballets: *Ragtime* (music by Stravinsky), *Symphony No. 5* (Schubert), *L'Heure Bleue* (Ravel) and *Over the Waves* (G. Hubbard Miller). Also included were two ballets by Balanchine, *The Four Temperaments* and *Concerto Barocco*, both staged by Francia, who was, and is, internationally respected for staging Balanchine ballets.

When *The Four Temperaments* was announced, one of Seattle's most knowledgeable arts critics upbraided Francia for presuming to present one of Balanchine's best ballets with dancers who were patently not adequate. Francia responded that Balanchine trusted her to stage his ballets (which, incidentally, he gave to PNB for no fee) if she had dancers capable of performing them, and the company did have such dancers. The critic scoffed, but after the first PND performance of *The Four Temperaments*, he rushed backstage to apologize to Francia and thank her for successfully staging the Balanchine classic. That was only one of many skirmishes in the battle to win over the media.

Although PND was performing its own work, the company was still subordinate to Seattle Opera, not only in organizational structure but also in administrative functions such as payroll, marketing and publicity. Kent and Francia sat at the feet of Glynn Ross, not figuratively but actually. One evening Ross asked them to stop by his home and, after seating himself in an easy chair, he told Kent and Francia to make themselves comfortable on the floor in front of him. He then told them that as general director he needed to know *everything* that was happening within PND. In Germany, Kent and Francia had been given a budget and then were free to stage ballets, no questions asked. Clearly the ground rules were different in Seattle. As they were leaving Ross's home that evening, Kent whispered to Francia, "Out of the frying pan. . . ."

Not long after that, Kent was in Ross's office discussing plans for PND's season-ending production of *Coppélia*. The economics of presenting an audience-pleasing comedic ballet for which PND already owned the costumes appealed to both men.

Francia and sons arrive in Seattle, July 1977. From left: Christopher, Ethan and Darren.

Kent: "I had called Robert O'Hearn in New York about designing new sets for our *Coppélia*. The one Millie [Melissa Hayden] had rented from Ballet West was tacky. When I told Glynn I was going to New York, he said I couldn't be flying off whenever I wanted. There was no money for that. Besides, he asked, why go to New York? When I said I was going to talk to O'Hearn about the *Coppélia* sets, Glynn really blew and said there was absolutely not a penny available for any new sets. So I told him that we'd received a grant for the sets, and that seemed to satisfy him. But it was a bald-faced lie. We didn't have a grant. Somehow it all worked out okay."

Kent choreographed *Coppélia* for the available number of costumes, and the ballet—new sets and all—did well enough at the box office to insure that PND would complete its 1977–78 year in the black, a result the board was adamant about achieving. The board was, in fact, sufficiently heartened by the success of the year to nearly double the budget for the 1978–79 fiscal year, going from slightly over $600,000 to $1 million. It also approved signing 24 dancers and six apprentices to contracts guaranteeing 30 weeks of rehearsal and performance.

By the summer of 1978, the Opera board was becoming increasingly disenchanted with Ross and with PND. Ross was renowned for his ability to pull financial rabbits out of a hat, but in recent months he had antagonized the Opera board by vigorously promoting his concept of a summer "Festival in the Forest" on land between Seattle and Tacoma that the Weyerhaeuser Company had agreed to donate. The Washington State Legislature, among others, thought the idea was a winner. Opera board members saw it as a money-sucking loser, and many felt the same about PND, which the Opera was backing administratively and which continued to exist only because the Opera did not demand payment of the loan it had made to PND when it started. (The loan was paid off within five years.) Finally, the Opera board said the ballet company was more a liability than a benefit to the Opera and should therefore be turned loose to fare for itself. Ross was the Opera's general director for only one more year.

Kent: "Of course, that's what we'd wanted all along: to be on our own. But still it was scary, because we lost a lot of support functions. But I thought—and told our board—if we can't stand on our own, we shouldn't be here."

New incorporation papers were drafted, and the company got the name it has lived with ever since: Pacific Northwest Ballet.

John E. Iverson, a Seattle attorney, became PNB's president, succeeding Winder, who became co-chairman with Phelps. Timothy Duncan left his job as head administrator of the Pennsylvania Ballet to become managing director of PNB, an appointment that

Opposite: Kent rehearses Over the Waves *with Jory Hancock and Ellen Troy.* Photo by David Cooper.

Following page: Kent and Francia are clearly of one mind during a dress rehearsal of Coppélia *at the Opera House in 1977.* PNB photo.

cheered PNB board members, who could hardly believe their luck in wooing away the top man from one of the nation's most highly regarded ballet companies. What they didn't know—and Duncan did—was that the Pennsylvania Ballet was approaching a financial crisis that would result in its severe downsizing and loss of prestige.

Kent: "Dave Winder effectively championed PNB's cause, and John Iverson was another very good president. He became our biggest cheerleader. He spent hours and hours cajoling people into attending performances and giving money. He was up front and courageous and very energetic. He really made a difference."

Iverson was no newcomer to the arts. He had taken dance classes during his years at the University of Washington and had performed in dances Robert Joffrey choreographed for musicals at Seattle's Aqua Theatre. His wife, Marli, had been a member of the Seattle Opera chorus and the Opera board.

"I was born in Seattle and had seen the growth of the arts here," Iverson recalled recently. "It was clear to me that the ballet needed to take a leap forward. A lot of things had to go into place then: revitalizing the board, increasing fund-raising, earning community recognition—the whole nine yards. So I just set about to do all those things. When I became president, we had a budget of just over a million dollars; when I left the presidency after two years, we had a budget of $2.2 million. Although we were growing by giant steps, the Seattle press was not paying attention to us. At a fund-raising party, I said to a reporter: 'We're the new kid on the artistic block.' That phrase hit the papers the next day, and ten years later it was still being quoted."

One of the most significant of those giant steps came in the form of a $150,000 grant from the National Endowment for the Arts, "signaling national recognition of the Northwest's commitment to ballet and new artistic leadership." The grant was for more money than the company's entire annual budget not many years before, and it had to be matched three-to-one, meaning that it would generate a total of $600,000. The matching-money requirement alarmed PNB board members.

Francia: "Some of them asked if we *had* to take it. They wanted to give it back! They were convinced they'd never be able to raise the $450,000 in matching money. But they did and we got the grant. It was *very* important to our development."

Around this time, a *Seattle Times* writer asked Kent what ambitions he had for PNB. "We have to be the best, we don't have any choice," said Kent. The writer asked the context of "best." "The best in the nation," said Kent. "And why not in the world?"

The reply seemed quixotic—then.

Pensive Kent during rehearsal. Photo by Jim Cummins.

Opposite: Kent as Dr. Coppelius with Michael Auer as

Franz in the 1983 production of Coppélia.

Photo by David Cooper.

CLASS VI

In Theatre Street, *one of the best books ever written about ballet, the legendary Russian ballerina Tamara Karsavina wrote: "I felt the sheer joy of movement and the determination to persevere. Instinct was to hold me on my path, till understanding came to prove the path a right one."* ❧ *The PNB female dancers communicate "the sheer joy of movement" in their vigorously athletic work "in the center," twirling and leaping and soaring with apparent ease in* grands jetés. *Now, as class nears its end, they again arrange themselves in casual lines. Francia speaks a few words softly and the dancers begin exercises in* port de bras, *carriage of the arms. They move slowly, gracefully through changes in arm position, complemented by traditionally specified movement of the rest of the body. They create a quiet, contemplative harmony. Individual and collective focus are achieved.* ❧ *"Port de bras and the line of the head and neck are really important to me," Francia says later. "Port de bras is also about breathing, about the importance of the upper body. And it's also a coming together of the dancers at the end of class."* ❧ *After warm mutual applause, Francia and the dancers disperse.* ❧ *"Francia is our mentor and our role model," says one of the dancers. "We always try to do our best when she teaches class. Her classes are demanding but always rewarding."* ❧ *"It's funny," says Francia. "When dancers retire, most of them think, 'Thank god, I won't have to do class anymore.' But in fact, that's what they miss most."*

Swan Lake to The Nutcracker

Two productions that were crucial in PNB's development are, coincidentally, Tchaikovsky's first and last ballets: *Swan Lake* (1876) and *The Nutcracker* (whose full title was *The Nutcracker and the Mouse King* at its premiere in St. Petersburg in 1892, the year before Tchaikovsky's death). The PNB production of *Swan Lake* in 1981 proved to the community (and to the PNB board) that the Seattle-based company was capable of using its own resources to create excellence in a major ballet; after the opening night of *Swan Lake*, the company never again felt the need to hire visiting stars. In 1983, the brand-new *Nutcracker* production, designed by Maurice Sendak, brought national praise to PNB and gave the company a splendid show that annually produces about one-third of the company's earned income. Kent and Francia collaborated on *Swan Lake*, she staging scenes with the traditional Petipa-Ivanov choreography and he creating new choreography for parts of the first and third acts and for all of the fourth act. Kent created an entirely new scenario and choreography for *The Nutcracker*.

The couple had staged a successful production of *Swan Lake* in Frankfurt, and they were confident they had the dancers to make *Swan Lake* a success for PNB. The ballet is one of the world's best known, a touchstone for any ballet company; it's also a mammoth undertaking that requires a big budget. Kent arranged to save money on the sets by using the Frankfurt designs and having copies made, but even though he cut corners, the production still represented a big financial risk.

"I had many moments of doubt about whether we could raise the money for *Swan Lake*," recalls John E. Iverson, who was board president at the time. "We had to find money to build the sets and 175 costumes. Our goal was a quarter of a million dollars. The production was scheduled for June of 1981, but I said if we didn't have the funds in hand by August 1980, we weren't going to do it. August came, and we didn't have all the money. But we did have some money and more was in the pipeline. The key to the whole thing was Roland Trafton of Safeco. He made one of the first big donations, and because he said yes, a number of big corporations and major private donors got in line."

Francia: "John [Iverson] was really behind us in taking on the challenge of *Swan Lake*. He was instrumental in spurring on the board."

Kent: "Even when we got into staging *Swan Lake*, there were still many concerns about doing the ballet. There was an influential woman in town who regularly complained that we didn't bring in enough guest stars. She said: 'We can't expect people to pay for high-priced tickets to see *our* dancers!' There was so much pressure to bring in stars for the opening night that I finally agreed. We brought out Gelsey Kirkland and Patrick Bissell from New York."

Opposite: Louise Nadeau in Swan Lake.
Photo by Ben Kerns.

Page 61: Patricia Barker and Ronn Tice rehearse as Francia watches. Photo by Kurt Smith.

Gelsey Kirkland. Seattle Times photo by Ann Yow.

Kirkland had been one of Francia's students at the School of American Ballet in New York, and she worked well with Francia in *Swan Lake* rehearsals. But by this time her stellar career was being undermined by her lifestyle and her prima-donna attitude. When she arrived in Seattle for *Swan Lake*, she brought with her (stuffed into a Bloomingdale's shopping bag) a red tutu from a *Don Quixote* production, and she was insistent that she was going to wear that *red* tutu in the *Black* Swan pas de deux. Kent convinced her agent to hide that red tutu, and Kirkland reluctantly went on dressed in black. At least she rehearsed. Bissell didn't.

Kent: "But when Patrick went out on the stage, he was brilliant. One of our girls fell flat on her fanny in the second act, and I felt it like a stab in the stomach. I knew I would hear about it from Jerry Sanford (a key board member), who called us the Fall Down Ballet Company. Then in the third act, during the Black Swan pas de deux, it came time for the famous 32 *fouettés*, which audiences think is the equivalent of walking a tightrope over Niagara Falls, and when the dancer succeeds, everybody applauds like crazy. Well, Gelsey was doing those *fouettés*, and I found myself thinking the unkind wish that she'd fall down so that everyone could see that star dancers fall, too. No sooner had I thought it than Gelsey fell. She went *splat!*—on her back with her legs up in the air and with a shouted expletive that's not in Tchaikovsky's score. The next night our own dancers, Deborah Hadley and Jory Hancock, danced a wonderful *Swan Lake*. Many of our board members came back on the second night to see the home dancers perform, and to a person they all said that our dancers were better than the big stars. After that, no one ever again suggested that we have guest artists."

The *Swan Lake* production was a huge success. Audiences loved it; critics loved it; board members loved it; and the box office loved the action it created. It would have been an unqualified triumph for the company, except for one detail. Several PNB staff members, aware that the *Swan Lake* production was a capital-letter Big Deal for the company, prepared a big, lavishly illustrated souvenir book that was given to board members and contributors. The cost of creating the book essentially erased the profit from the *Swan Lake* performances. "That would not happen today" is Kent's curt critique.

A recession in the early 1980s had a crimping effect on virtually all aspects of Seattle's economy. For the first time in its history (including the PND days) PNB had a deficit, and that violated the organization's cardinal rule: *Always be in the black!* Travis Keeler, who had succeeded his friend John Iverson as president of PNB, took the deficit personally, as if he had been an defective leader by running PNB into red ink. Because of sharp cutbacks in the staff, board members were coming into the PNB office and performing staff functions. The size of the deficit? $15,000!

Kent called Richard LeBlond, the president of the San Francisco Ballet, and asked him to come to Seattle and talk with the PNB board. When LeBlond told board members that a $15,000 deficit was mere chicken feed and gave them encouragement for what PNB was doing, they relaxed a bit. But the recession continued, as did PNB's anemic finances.

Kent and Francia are, typically, of a mind about Keeler: "Travis was president at a difficult time for PNB. Even though he never would take any credit for himself and never even believed he did a good job, he was in fact an excellent president." (At a board meeting in spring 1997 when a major endowment campaign was being discussed, Keeler spoke eloquently in support of the campaign and pledged a generous financial contribution, saying he felt honored to support PNB.)

When Tim Duncan resigned as PNB's managing director to accept a similar position in San Francisco, his assistant, Margo Donaldson, succeeded him; shortly afterward Jerome Sanford, long a key board member and a recent retiree from Boeing, became the company's executive director. Then, after a reorganization, Sanford became PNB's first paid president; Arthur H. Mazzola succeeded his friends Iverson and Keeler in a position that was now called chairman; and Phelps became chairman emeritus.

While the leadership played organizational musical chairs, the company was preparing and presenting a new production of *The Nutcracker*, a ballet that, during every Christmas season, functions as a cash cow for virtually every American ballet company. Lew Christensen's *Nutcracker* had served PNB well almost from the company's beginning, but mounting their own new production of the holiday chestnut had never been far from Kent and Francia's thoughts. The success of *Swan Lake* emboldened them to plan seriously for the new production. One Sunday in 1981, Francia read a *New York Times*

Linnette Hitchin and PNB dancers in Swan Lake.

Photo by David Cooper.

Maurice Sendak (left) and Kent in the Opera House at a dress rehearsal of The Nutcracker. *PNB photo.*

review of a Houston production of Mozart's opera *The Magic Flute* that was designed by Maurice Sendak, the author and illustrator of many best-selling children's books. She suggested to Kent that it would be "incredible to have Sendak's kind of imagination" at work on a new *Nutcracker*. Kent forthwith called Sendak at his home in Connecticut and arranged to meet him in New York City.

Kent: "I'd never met Maurice, and he was reluctant at first. He said he'd been worried that I was going to be some big-ego ballet freak."

Sendak: "I liked Kent a lot, right from the beginning. But I felt the same way as I had when I was asked to do *The Magic Flute*. Although I loved opera, I didn't then know anything about opera design, and I sure didn't know anything about ballet before I met Kent. Besides, I thought *Nutcracker* was a snoozer, a holiday turkey."

Kent: "I told Maurice I didn't want to do just another *Nutcracker*. I wanted to start over and completely rethink and redo the whole ballet."

Sendak: "That intrigued me. We spent a wonderful afternoon talking about the ballet, exploring the dark side of *Nutcracker*, the erotic side that makes the original tale by E.T.A. Hoffmann so fascinating. Clara is obviously having a sexual dream. Hormones are surging through her, and she finally wins her prince. Seen from Hoffmann's point of view, the story has a logical through-line. The more Kent and I talked, the more I got excited about the idea, and I agreed to design the ballet—sets and costumes. It didn't take any arm-twisting by Kent. I was either very naïve or just plain stupid to try to design a full-length ballet when I didn't know anything about ballet."

When Kent told the board that Sendak was interested in designing *The Nutcracker*, there was a great flurry. The board members were, in Kent's words, "so excited that they thought money would fall out of the trees." Some board members suggested that the production would be an irresistible magnet for foundation and corporate money; others said that Sendak himself or some of his rich friends would surely put up substantial funds for the show. Some even suggested that PNB could get rich on royalties from *Nutcracker* dolls and related novelties. Everybody thought somebody else was going to fund the ballet.

After multiple trips by Kent to New York and by Sendak to Seattle, designs were completed and sent out for bid. During one of the New York visits, Kent introduced Sendak to Lincoln Kirstein, a tall patrician man who had founded the School of American Ballet and the New York City Ballet for Balanchine. Kirstein inspected Sendak and said: "Now I can see why all the characters in your books are short and stocky." (In fact, Sendak bears a striking resemblance to *The Nutcracker's* title character, whose face has appeared on PNB posters since 1983.)

Kirstein's chill melted when he saw Sendak's designs. In a note to Sheffield Phelps in June 1983, Kirstein wrote: "Kent Stowell has let me see the designs for your *Nutcracker* by Maurice Sendak. I thought they were absolutely magnificent and I was filled with violent greed and envy. On December 17, we [the New York City Ballet] are dancing our 1,000th performance [of *The Nutcracker*] and I only wish we had such a beautiful and carefully planned treatment. This is not luck,—but the operation of the analytical intelligence, a rare phenomenon. May I extend my heartiest congratulations."

From various grants and support from local foundations, corporations and individuals, about $200,000 was initially raised for the project, and the board authorized Stowell to spend that amount to begin building *The Nutcracker*. Randall G. Chiarelli, PNB's accomplished lighting designer and technical director (whom everyone calls Rico), was orchestrating the process.

Kent: "It was like preparations for the Gulf War. Things were being organized all over the country. Some of the scenery was painted in Toronto, some built in San Francisco. The costumes were made in New York and San Francisco. The tree was made in New York. We zipped through the $200,000, and our suppliers needed more money for materials. It was a hectic time, trying to realize a dream without falling apart during the process of creation. After we ran out of money, the next board meeting was a knockdown, drag-out affair. People were standing up and screaming and leaving in disgust. We were all really on a tightrope. I met with [PNB president] Jerry Sanford, and with all the bills and bids coming in, the total cost looked to be about $600,000, which was an enormous amount for our organization then—three times as much as for *Swan Lake*. Jerry said, 'I absolutely won't have anything to do with this. It's way out of hand for PNB.' I stopped by the box office and asked how many advance tickets we'd sold for *Nutcracker*. It was something like 13,000 tickets and we still had more than two months to go. Then I asked how many *Nutcracker* tickets we'd sold a year ago at this time. It was

Seth Belliston is behind the mask in The Nutcracker.

Photo by Rick Dean.

something like 1,100. So I went to Jerry and the board and said: 'Who's going to tell the individuals, corporations and foundations that have already given us $200,000 that we aren't going to do the *Nutcracker* they helped pay for? Who's going to call the people that have bought 13,000 tickets and tell them there's no new *Nutcracker*?' I told them: 'If we do that, we're dead. We'll never be able to raise another cent in this town for anything.' Everybody swallowed hard."

Francia: "It was a horrible board meeting. Kent had to leave to go to rehearsal, and I was left there with the board. They were very fixed on the idea of my working to stage the Christensen *Nutcracker* as a backup possibility, while Kent was choreographing the new *Nutcracker*. I had to explain the impossible logistics of that: the dancers, the kids, the parents and so on. But the board was very serious about our doing Kent's new first act and Christensen's old second act."

Kent: "Finally the board realized that we were in so deep that we could do nothing but go ahead. There was cursing, but the board voted to move ahead. The ticket campaign began and we sold so many tickets that we were able to pay for the new *Nutcracker* that first year. In 1982, we did $600,000 on the old *Nutcracker*. On the new *Nutcracker* in 1983, we did twice as much—$1.2 million. We paid for the production and had money in the bank. That went down like honey for the board members. But that *Nutcracker* marked the end of PNB as a naïve, innocent organization."

The days leading to *The Nutcracker's* opening night were taut with stressed-out nerves and strewn with production roadblocks. One of Sendak's design concepts was to expand the stage objects out of scale to suggest a child's view of the world. At the PNB warehouse, Sendak was shown one of the two clocks he had designed. "My god," said Sendak, "it's so big! Show me the smaller clock." Rico told him: "Maurice, this *is* the smaller clock!" Later, at dress rehearsal, a Sendak-designed toy box turned out to be so big that there was no place for it on the stage, and it had to be scrapped.

Sendak had also created a design to be painted on the floor. At dress rehearsal it was discovered that the out-of-town shop that built the floor had used the wrong covering, with a surface so slippery that the dancers couldn't keep their feet. That floor was scrapped and a floor with the proper surface was put down. Painters started at 11 P.M., worked through the night and finished Sendak's design at 7 o'clock on the morning of opening night.

Mazzola, chairman of the deeply worried PNB board, recalls an incident from *The Nutcracker's* opening night: "I had a little time to kill before going to a pre-performance dinner for board members and friends. I was thinking about what I was going to say at

Alaina Albertson and Michael Auer rehearse at the Good Shepherd Center, with Rico Chiarelli looking on. PNB photo.

Opposite: Anne Derieux as the Peacock and Uko Gorter as Pasha in PNB's Nutcracker. *Photo by Ben Kerns.*

that gathering. I picked up a newspaper and absently began reading the personals, something I never, ever read. There in the personals were lists of people begging for tickets to *The Nutcracker*. People were offering as much as $125 for a pair of tickets—in 1983 that was a lot of money. I thought that if there ever was a question about the success of our roll of the dice, this answers it. I read those personals aloud at the dinner that evening, and everybody felt better."

The Stowell-Sendak *Nutcracker* was a super-success for PNB, regularly inspiring standing ovations from sellout audiences. The critics flipped adjective over adverb in praise of the old chestnut's new incarnation. *Newsweek* told readers that *The Nutcracker* alone was worth the trip to Seattle.

Sendak has warm recollections of the experience: "Doing *Nutcracker* was like being a designer and trainee at the same time, with Kent and Francia teaching me. They're expert teachers and very convincing. Everyone in the company was very helpful. I loved the whole experience, and I fell in love with the dancers. When production complications came up and I was feeling hassled, I'd go watch the dancers in class. That had a remarkable calming and focusing effect. I don't know what's going on physically or psychically with dancers, but it has to be very complex and, I think, very painful much of the time. It's their whole life, and they have to give their all always, because it's a short life. They've got to bloom very quickly."

The new *Nutcracker* production marked the first PNB appearance of Stewart Kershaw, a British conductor who had been engaged as the company's musical director and conductor; he had worked with Kent and Francia off and on since 1972 during their years in Germany. A native of Oxford, England, Kershaw had a blue-ribbon education at home and abroad and had conducted such famed companies as the Royal Ballet in London and the Paris Opera Ballet. The final *Nutcracker* performance in 1996 marked the 360th time Kershaw conducted that ballet for PNB.

Over the years, *The Nutcracker* has been a consistent winner for PNB, both in earning money and in bringing new audiences to the ballet. In 1996, gross receipts for *The Nutcracker* exceeded $3 million for the first time, an amount representing nearly a third of the company's earned income in its 1996–97 fiscal year.

Maurice Sendak (left), Stewart Kershaw (center) and Kent take a curtain call at the premiere of their Nutcracker *in 1983.* PNB photo.

Opposite: Maria Chapman, Kim Smith (in mirror) and Kristie George prepare for a performance of Kent's Nutcracker. Photo by Kurt Smith.

CLASS VII

Today's class is for about 30 youngsters, a racial and ethnic rainbow of kids dressed in ballet's traditional black and white. They're participants in PNB's DanceChance program, which gives inner-city elementary school kids an all-expenses-paid opportunity to learn ballet basics and, if they show talent and motivation, to continue training in the PNB School. ❦ The guest teachers today are Naomi Gedo Johnson-Washington and Dr. Zakariya Sao Diouf, experts in African music and dance. They have come to PNB from their home in the Bay Area primarily to assist choreographer Val Caniparoli in rehearsing his ballet Lambarena, *which uses ballet and African movements with a score that blends African rhythms and melodies with music by Bach. But now they're teaching class. ❦ Johnson-Washington, a native of Nigeria, gives the youngsters clear, patient instruction on how to move to the complex rhythms drummed by Sao Diouf, former director of the Mali Ensemble. The kids are obviously trying hard, and it's also obvious that most are responding with two left feet to the exotic movements and the rhythms. Johnson-Washington, who has a sunrise smile that illuminates the studio, works gently with the kids, encouraging even the most errant attempts. The youngsters spin, jump, shake, leap through the movements she indicates. As class progresses, about half of them begin to get the hang of it. They return her smile. ❦ Later the youngsters tiptoe into Studio C and sit on the floor in front of the mirrored wall. They watch wide-eyed as Caniparoli rehearses PNB dancers. The kids recognize the rhythms; they've just learned them. After 15 minutes, the youngsters collectively begin a movement common among young audiences: the* pas de squirmée. *As they file out, a PNB teacher, gesturing toward the rehearsing dancers, asks one of the young girls: "You think you can do that?" "No!" is the quick answer. "I'll bet you can—someday," says the teacher.*

The Center at the Center

One of the truisms about nonprofit arts organizations is that they move inexorably from one financial crisis to the next. After the *Nutcracker* crisis not only had been resolved but had resulted in a giant step forward for PNB, the organization confronted a new crisis that had been developing as the company grew. The Good Shepherd Center was adequate in PNB's early years, but the old stone building was becoming increasingly cramped and was inhibiting the company's growth, both quantitatively and qualitatively. When PNB staff and board members seriously focused attention on this problem in 1984, little did they know that its solution would take nine years and $11 million.

In mid-1983, the PNB board took an important step toward professional administration by hiring Jerome Sanford to be the company's first paid president. During the 1982–83 season, Sanford had served as PNB's executive director, while Sheffield Phelps was chairman. In organizational restructuring in 1984, Phelps became chairman emeritus (a position he still holds) and Sanford became president; as such, he was instrumental in maneuvering PNB out of the red and into the black. It had become clear that PNB was a big, growing business that needed a fully professional staff with administrative expertise equal to the company's artistic expertise. When Sanford became occupied with consulting work in Canada, the board conducted a national search and hired Arthur Jacobus, who served as the company's president and CEO from late 1984 until 1993, forming with Kent and Francia the PNB's executive triumvirate, with all three reporting directly to the board. Jacobus came to Seattle from Oakland, where he had been general manager of the Oakland Symphony for five years. Prior to that, he had served for more than two decades as a bandmaster for the U.S. Navy. When he left PNB, it was to return to the Bay Area to become executive director of the San Francisco Ballet.

Jacobus recalls his arrival at PNB: "What I came to was a highly respected company, rather young and with not very well developed organizational processes and staffing, but there was a good foundation on which to work. Over time, because of the increasing prestige of the company and the increasing ability to sell tickets and raise funds, we were able to build a strong administrative staff." Jacobus was clear in his priorities: "Quality is what we're all about. In order for that to continue, however, the organization must be run in a businesslike way, although it is not a business. A business exists to make money. We don't exist to make money. We make money so that we can make great art." Jacobus was PNB's top administrator during the years of its greatest growth, and he played a crucial role in the development of a splendid new home for PNB.

Various sites and construction possibilities for the new home had been examined and rejected by PNB officials by fall 1984 when Ewen Dingwall, the director of Seattle

Opposite: Paul Gibson and Kimberly Davey taking class with the company in the Phelps Center's Studio C. Photo by Kurt Smith.

Page 73: Zakariya Sao Diouf and Naomi Gedo Johnson-Washington in rehearsal for Lambarena *with Ariana Lallone. Choreographer Val Caniparoli is mirrored behind Sao Diouf.* Photo by Kurt Smith.

Center, suggested that they consider renovating the Exhibition Hall, which had been built at Seattle Center for the 1962 World's Fair. Located between the Opera House and the Seattle Center Playhouse (since remodeled into the Intiman Playhouse), the Exhibition Hall in 1984 was an underused relic of the World's Fair, with a faceless brick facade and a spacious interior that could charitably be described as utilitarian. A major remodeling of the building would give Seattle Center another jewel in its urban-park crown and provide PNB with a new, much larger home, a central location and a direct interior walkway to its performance space, a luxury enjoyed by few ballet companies.

As it stood in 1984, the Exhibition Hall interior was an expansive column-free space with a 40-foot ceiling. Dingwall's idea was to cut the space in half horizontally, with the upper portion becoming PNB's new home and the lower portion remaining exhibit space. Seattle architect Gordon Walker worked out the design, following guidelines formulated early on by Kent, Francia and other PNB staff members. Christopher Miller, PNB's director of operations and project manager for the extensive remodeling, lists those guidelines: "1) *Make the art form evident.* We wanted everyone who experienced the building, both interior and exterior, to know immediately that its function was about making dance and making dancers. The design must make visible and celebrate the work of the artists; 2) *Enhance the understanding and working relationships among the various components of the organization.* We wanted to insure that everyone perceived the role and importance that each individual working here had in achieving the mission of PNB. We made conscious design choices to juxtapose various 'non-related' spaces adjacent to one another so folks working in those spaces encountered one another throughout the working day."

Because of the time needed for planning and raising capital funds, construction didn't begin until March 1991. After being halted for seven months while additional money was raised, construction was completed, and in January 1993 PNB moved into its new home, named in honor of its longtime leader Sheffield Phelps and his late wife, Patricia, who was in effect the patron saint of the PNB School. The 52,300-square-foot facility has seven studios, three of which are used primarily by the performing company and four by the PNB School; the largest studio measures 60 feet by 65 feet, which allows the company to rehearse in a space as large as the area they use on the Opera House stage. All of the studios have wooden "sprung" floors constructed in a basket-weave design to cushion the dancers' impact.

Sheffield and Patricia Phelps. Photo by Chris Bennion.

Opposite: Seth Belliston and Kim Smith practice the Snow pas de deux *before a* Nutcracker *performance at the Seattle Opera House.* Photo by Kurt Smith.

The Phelps Center houses administrative, artistic, production and school offices, along with company, school and faculty dressing rooms, physical therapy room, music and video library, shoe storage room, archival room, lounge area for company and staff, conference room, board room, and costume shop and its related spaces—laundry, supply and wardrobe.

That list does not even hint at the spacious, airy wonder of the Phelps Center. It is surely among the best performing-arts facilities in the world. Everything necessary for making dance and dancers is there (except a scene shop/storage warehouse, which is located a few miles away). Because of the abundance of interior and exterior windows and open space, dancers and dancing are always visible, and during school hours the building is thronged with dancers of all ages, sizes and shapes.

Immediately inside the front door of the Phelps Center is a wide staircase. Ascending those stairs, which open onto the bright expansiveness of the Center, stirs in some visitors feelings of awe and reverence similar to those evoked when entering a cathedral. The Phelps Center is a cathedral of dance. And cathedrals don't come cheap. To create the Phelps Center and begin a modest endowment fund, PNB raised $11 million, by far the organization's biggest fund-raising effort to that date.

"For it to succeed, it had to be an all-out effort by the entire board and staff," recalls Wendy Griffin, who with Ken Hatch co-chaired the Phelps Center capital fund drive and who was board chairman in the years prior to its opening. "At that time, PNB was probably not prioritized very high among Seattle arts institutions. That was natural because it hadn't been around very long. But the fact that *The Nutcracker* was so tremendously successful inspired not only the board but the community, because the company had demonstrated its ability and its right to stand with other major cultural institutions in Seattle and to have its own home. There's no mystery about how you raise money. People ask people for money. They give if you're passionate and committed to your cause and if they believe you."

CLASS VIII

Today's class, part of PNB's Bravo! Ballet program, which is designed to introduce students to ballet, is in the gymnasium of Rainier Beach High School in south Seattle. Phil Otto, a retired PNB soloist and now a teacher in the PNB School, greets a group of 15 youngsters: mostly African-Americans, several of Asian heritage, one Caucasian. The students look embarrassed, even a bit suspicious. Three of the boys, football and basketball players, don't hide their what-am-I-doing-here aloofness. ❧ *Otto, tall and muscular and obviously a fit athlete, explains and demonstrates ballet's five positions of the feet. The kids follow his lead, and most lose their balance trying to make their feet turn out. The student athletes merely shuffle their feet casually. Otto names and demonstrates a few ballet steps:* tendu, glissade, jeté. *The students tentatively try the steps and giggle at their clumsiness.* ❧ *Fast-forward 40 minutes. Bouncy, rhythmic music is playing. The students are in two lines, moving forward in unison, doing a combination of steps Otto has taught them. The kids are now moving confidently, smiling, obviously pleased with what they're doing. Dancing! Two of the girls incorporate hip-hop moves into the steps. The three jocks are really into the dance; their resistance has given way to intense concentration and the joy of achievement. Look, they seem to say, I can do ballet!* ❧ *Otto congratulates all the kids on their progress and tells them when he'll be back. The youngsters, entirely unaware of the tradition of dancers' applauding the teacher at the end of class, spontaneously and unanimously applaud Otto. He beams. The kids beam.* ❧ *"I wish we could do this regularly with PNB," says a flushed teacher who has been working out along with the students. "This is just terrific for the kids. We don't have anything like this in the school."*

Art at Home and Abroad

It's impossible to make an objective assessment of PNB's artistic qualities, but the company's artistic development is real and documented. When PNB performed at the Brooklyn Academy of Music in 1984, the reputation-making New York critics gave it mixed reviews, but when the company appeared at New York's City Center in 1996, the critics raved about it and hailed its ascension to major national status.

By the usual American way of establishing pecking order (that is, quantitatively), PNB's $11 million annual operating budget places its national ranking behind the New York City Ballet ($34.6 million), American Ballet Theatre ($21.5 million), San Francisco Ballet ($19 million) and Boston Ballet ($16.8 million). Locally, PNB's $11 million operating budget puts it in a dead heat with Seattle Opera as Seattle's largest performing-arts organization, but the local economic impact of PNB, which doesn't import expensive stars, is greater than that of Seattle Opera, whose imported performers leave town with substantial fees.

Placing PNB in its proper qualitative niche is a much more dicey proposition, since that would involve matters of taste, to say nothing of parochialism and assorted other chauvinist puffery. Still, it's not going out on a splintered limb to say that PNB now ranks with the New York City Ballet, the New York–based American Ballet Theatre and the ballet companies in San Francisco, Boston and Houston. How the order of excellence among them is judged probably depends on where the judge lives.

Over its 25 years, PNB has presented 120 ballets, 68 of which are still in the company's active repertoire, which has three principal divisions: 25 ballets by Balanchine, 24 by Kent and 19 by other 20th-century choreographers, nearly all of them still living and working. The last category will be significantly expanded in the 1997–98 season, when the company will present ten world premieres and four Seattle premieres, all by 20th-century choreographers. In the last 20 years, PNB has presented ballets by 63 different choreographers.

The large presence of Balanchine in the repertoire has prompted some in the dance world to label PNB a Balanchine clone company, a claim seemingly supported by more facts: both Kent and Francia danced for Balanchine in his prime at the New York City Ballet; Francia is one of the world's top experts in staging Balanchine ballets; and Kent's choreography shows Balanchine's influence. Although they proudly admit Balanchine's influence (as what contemporary American ballet artistic director wouldn't?), Kent and Francia dismiss the clone label. They contend that the PNB company has its own identity, its own "look." Francia says: "The PNB style is very clean, clear and honest."

Opposite: Francia staging Balanchine's Theme and Variations *for the Kirov Ballet in St. Petersburg, Russia.*

Page 81: Phil Otto teaches ballet basics at Rainier Beach High School. Photo by Kurt Smith.

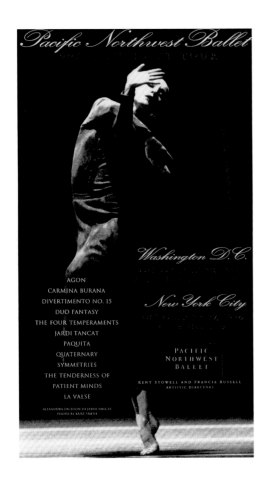

Poster for the 1996 East Coast tour, showing Alexandra

Dickson in Jardí Tancat.

Opposite: Deborah Hadley and Benjamin Houk in
The Tragedy of Romeo and Juliet. *Photo by Ben Kerns.*

In 1985 PNB mounted a production of *A Midsummer Night's Dream*, one of Balanchine's rare full-length ballets, and the company closed its 1996–97 season with a sumptuous and witty new production of *Midsummer* with sets and costumes by Broadway designer Martin Pakledinaz, staging by Francia and lighting design by PNB's Rico Chiarelli. It marked the first time a full-length Balanchine ballet had been given an entirely new physical production, and the $600,000 ballet was cheered by audiences and critics, as well as by representatives of the Balanchine Trust. So much for cloning.

In addition to *Swan Lake* and *The Nutcracker*, Kent's full-length ballets include *Coppélia*, which he staged in 1978 (at the end of his first PNB season) in an effort to economize, because the company already owned costumes for the ballet; *The Tragedy of Romeo and Juliet*, a 1987 production that many consider his masterpiece; and *Cinderella*, which he staged in the 1993–94 season, along with a major new production of *Carmina Burana*, as a way of proclaiming that PNB wasn't going to relax after moving into the Phelps Center. At home and on the road, *Cinderella* has proved to be a money-in-the-bank ballet for PNB; also popular is Kent's production of Stravinsky's *Firebird*, which the company premiered at the Kennedy Center in 1989.

Prokofiev's *Romeo and Juliet* is a staple of most major ballet companies, but for *The Tragedy of Romeo and Juliet*, Kent and PNB music director Stewart Kershaw pieced together a new score using some of Tchaikovsky's less well known music (*not* including the popular *Romeo and Juliet Fantasy Overture*). The evocative and eminently danceable music heightens Kent's intimate approach to the famous love story. Unlike Balanchine's Shakespeare-inspired ballet, *A Midsummer Night's Dream*, which tells the story in broad strokes in the first act and then has a second act of pure dance, Kent's retelling of a Shakespeare tale has a strong narrative through-line from beginning to end. Deborah Hadley, the accomplished dancer on whom Kent created Juliet, cites the ballet as the pinnacle of her distinguished career; her high opinion of the ballet is shared by many dancers, critics and balletomanes.

Central to PNB's artistic philosophy is this comment by Francia: "The repertoire has to be revitalized. There have to be new works. We have to keep up with the times. We have to stimulate our dancers and our audiences. Many on the board and staff think we ought to repeat our successes. But we can't do things so often that they don't remain vitally interesting."

Touring is also of crucial importance to PNB. "Dancers need performances" is one of Kent's recurrent comments, and with PNB restricted in performance dates at the Opera House by having to share that facility with the Seattle Symphony, Seattle Opera and

PACIFIC NORTHWEST BALLET ✳ KENT STOWELL AND FRANCIA RUSSELL, ARTISTIC DIRECTORS

FIREBIRD

CHOREOGRAPHED BY KENT STOWELL ✳ MUSIC BY IGOR STRAVINSKY
SETS BY MING CHO LEE ✳ COSTUMES DESIGNED BY THEONI ALDREDGE
KENNEDY CENTER OPERA HOUSE ✳ SEPTEMBER 26-OCTOBER 1,1989
TICKETS AT THE BOX OFFICE, TICKETRON OR CALL INSTANT-CHARGE (202) 857-0900 467-4600 AFTER SEPT 22 634-7201 · GROUP SALES 254-3770 ·INFO

The Theoni Aldredge Firebird *poster for PNB's 1989*

appearance at the Kennedy Center Opera House.

other community groups, touring has been a way to get the company's dancers before audiences.

"Touring is a definite priority," says Allen C. Shoup, who became chairman of PNB's board in mid-1996. "If you have world-class dancers, they have a right to appear on the world stage to reinforce their efforts and reward them. Touring gives a company credibility. If we tour around the world and show the world what we have, then people back home will be that much more supportive of us."

The payoff from touring was obvious after PNB's week of performances in October 1996 at City Center in New York City. The company's success, haloed in glowing reviews from New York critics, led virtually directly to several large grants from national foundations and record-breaking attendance for the company's subsequent performances in Seattle in the 1996–97 season.

"The New York trip put PNB on the map as a player," says David F. Hill, PNB's president. "If I'm reading about how wonderful PNB is in the *Wall Street Journal*, that's pretty terrific. And that excitement carried over. I'd never been hounded for *Nutcracker* tickets before, but after New York, I got lots of calls from people eager to see *Nutcracker*."

The New York trip also included a startling incident that sent shock waves through the whole PNB organization and that surely will be the stuff of legend for years to come. More about that later.

PNB's touring history has followed, not surprisingly, the same path as the organization's overall development: from modest to larger, to larger still, and finally to world-class ambition. The company's first out-of-town performances were of *The Nutcracker* in Vancouver, British Columbia, in 1979. In subsequent years, PNB has returned to Vancouver nine times with various works from its repertoire. In 1981, the company made the first of two tours to Alaska.

The company's first genuinely daunting tour appearance was its premiere visit to New York City in April 1984 for performances at the Brooklyn Academy of Music. The reviews from the New York critics were encouraging pats on the back followed by chilly evaluations of the company's strengths and deficiencies. Bearing in mind that any New York City appearance not savaged by the critics is a success, the company took positive vibes away from New York, along with an invitation to dance at the Spoleto USA Festival in Charleston, South Carolina, a few months later.

In 1984, PNB made the first of five visits to Minneapolis, where it was so well received that a Seattle-Minneapolis ballet cooperative program was seriously explored, although it was never consummated. Aspen, Berkeley, Yakima, Tacoma and Portland were added to the company tour itinerary in 1985, and in 1987 PNB received the first of four invitations to dance at the Kennedy Center. Alan M. Kriegsman, the dean of dance critics in Washington, D.C., called the company "classy and distinguished . . . a revelation . . . one of the nation's outstanding classical companies . . . the dancers are conspicuously attractive and well-trained."

In 1990 the company made the first of three tours to Hawaii, over the years performing a large repertoire including two full-length ballets, *Coppélia* and *A Midsummer Night's Dream*. The company toured Arizona with *Cinderella*, a production that was also successful in Edmonton and Calgary, Canada, and at the tony Orange County Performing Arts Center in California; in that state, the company has also performed in Los Angeles and Berkeley and at the Stern Grove Festival in the Bay Area.

In October 1995, the company traveled to Australia to open the Melbourne Festival of the Arts. The Australian tour inspired such paeans as the following in *Dance Magazine*: "There is little doubt that this intelligent, vivacious, wholly dedicated group of young American artists has captured the hearts of local balletomanes."

All of that touring can be viewed as prelude to the main event: performing before the make-or-break New York critics in the heart of Manhattan at City Center, the theatre where Kent and Francia danced when they were in Balanchine's New York City Ballet. The New York engagement followed a return visit to the Kennedy Center, but unlike the Washington, D.C., performances, for which the company received a fee, PNB was on its own in the Big Apple, footing all the bills for transportation, hall rental, orchestra musicians, stagehands, lodging and food, advertising, and numerous other expenses. You name it, it cost. Plenty. After all the red ink was pooled, PNB officials came up with an estimate (later proved accurate) that the performance week at City Center would cost the company $275,000. That number made the PNB board think hard.

Susan Brotman, PNB chairman when the trip was approved, says: "Touring has always been the subject of a lot of differing opinions among board members. Touring costs money, and we have to wonder if we're taking money away from what we might better offer at home. Going to New York City was a big risk. The decision was made easy, however, because Kent and Francia felt so strongly about going at that time. They thought, and finally the board thought, that if we didn't go, we would lose the ability to make the next big step in our reputation."

Strong support for the New York trip came from board member Bob Braun, a long-time dedicated supporter of PNB. Those at the board meeting when the trip finances were being discussed recall Braun saying: "We have the money for the trip. We're not a

Julie Tobiason and Uko Gorter in Coppélia.

Photo by Ben Kerns.

Ross Yearsley and Louise Nadeau in Balanchine's
Divertimento No. 15. Photo by Kurt Smith.

bank! If Kent and Francia think it's important to take the company to New York, it's not just the *right* thing to finance the trip; we have an *obligation* to spend the money for what's important."

The New York trip was essentially a referendum on Kent and Francia's two decades of leadership of PNB. The 1984 trip to Brooklyn brought PNB a kind of positive shrug from the critics, but at City Center in Manhattan, it would be thumbs-up or thumbs-down. And if it were the latter, the company would be seriously demoralized, the board would to certain to avoid future risks, and Kent and Francia on their own initiative might pack for who-knows-where.

The City Center engagement was, of course, a triumph. While not giving up their sacred duty to find fault, the critics practically swooned. Anna Kisselgoff of the *New York Times* wrote that PNB "would stand out in the richest of [New York] seasons." She noted that Kent and Francia "have done wonders with grooming [PNB] for the national status to which it so deservedly aspires." She was wowed by the performance of Balanchine's *Divertimento No. 15*, staged by Francia: "It took one's breath away and defined how far the company has come. . . . In Ms. Russell's glistening production, Mozart's clarity is matched with a clarity of detailed footwork. . . . In *Quaternary*, Mr. Stowell proves again how well he choreographs for his own dancers."

In the *Wall Street Journal*, Joan Acocella wrote: "The PNB dancers have a number of striking qualities—highly arched feet, free, buoyant thighs—but the thing that defines them is their musicality. These people are as musical as tap dancers. They don't just dance on the beat; they dance in it, through it. And when they have to choose between correctness of form and fidelity to the music—such things happen—they favor the music. They have been trained that way."

No shilly-shallying for William Deresiewicz of London's *Financial Times*: "The visit of Seattle's Pacific Northwest Ballet was the dance event of the season in New York. . . . The company's style is magnificently vibrant and proud. The carriage is easy yet taut with energy, the gaze lifted and alert. Hips are square and midsections are strong, making for great purity of shape and directness of attack. Phrasing is meticulously sharp. Most lovely are the PNB arms: radiant, full, exquisitely modeled. . . . In all, a consummately finished company, handsome to its fingertips, elegant without a hint of fuss."

The most touching comment came from veteran dance critic Deborah Jowitt, who ended her positive review by saying: "I'd forgotten what it was like to fall in love with a ballet company."

Over the next few months, the effect of the New York success was apparent at PNB's Seattle box office, where new records were set for *The Nutcracker*, the mixed-repertoire programs and *Midsummer*. New grants arrived. In direct response to PNB's success with Balanchine ballets in New York, the Wiegand Foundation provided $125,000 for staging Balanchine's *Ballet Imperial* in PNB's 1997–98 season. Philip Morris, which had resisted PNB's past grant requests because it said it didn't fund "regional" companies, came through with $25,000. And from the Lila Wallace–Reader's Digest Fund came $400,000 for audience development. So much for the $275,000 New York deficit! Best investment PNB ever made!

The startling incident referred to earlier occurred on the company's third night at City Center. There are as many variations of the story as there are persons who tell it. As near as can be determined, here's what happened:

Only a few minutes into the first ballet of the evening, Balanchine's *Divertimento No. 15*, Kent popped out of his seat, raced down the aisle, leaned into the orchestra pit and shouted at the conductor: "It's too fast, Stewart!" Then Kent wheeled and bolted out of the theatre. There was audible shock among audience members and the musicians in the pit, some of whom stopped playing. But conductor Stewart Kershaw kept up the beat and the show went on. Linnette Hitchin, who was alone on stage dancing the first variation in *Divertimento No. 15*, didn't miss a step, and the entire ballet was completed. At intermission, Kershaw threatened not to continue the evening's performance unless he received a public apology. Rico Chiarelli, PNB's lighting designer and technical director, and Otto Neubert, PNB's ballet master, convinced Kershaw that holding out for an apology would further gum up an already sticky situation. So the conductor and the company went on with the program—two more Balanchine ballets. Each time Kershaw took a bow, the audience gave him a rousing ovation.

Patricia Barker and Ulrik Wivel in Carmina Burana.

Photo by David Cooper.

Linnette Hitchin in Petipa's Paquita.

Photo by Ben Kerns.

The incident was duly reported in the New York newspapers—and on the front page of the *Seattle Times*. Anna Kisselgoff commented in the *New York Times*: "There is nothing like a mom-and-pop approach to running a ballet company, and at least here was a director who cared passionately about his dancers."

Kent recalls: "I called the company together the next morning on stage and apologized to the dancers. I told them I blew it and I was sorry it happened. I apologized to Stewart, and I said to him: 'What are we going to do about it? You can't put the toothpaste back in the tube. Let's go on.'"

Kent's disruption of a performance of prime importance shocked the dancers and even angered some. There were those throughout the organization who thought the bond of trust between Kent and them had been broken. There were rumors that when the company returned to Seattle, Kent would take time off for an extended period; this soothed some who felt he needed the time to get squared away. But after two days' absence, Kent was back on the scene at the Phelps Center. Subsequently there was a lot of tiptoeing on eggshells, and although seemingly everyone associated with the company wanted to talk about the incident, all insisted on confidentiality; moreover, there were so many different versions of the story and its ramifications that it would take a novel of Jamesian heft to explore all the nuances. If any bond between Kent and the dancers was in fact broken, it was not apparent in the company's subsequent performances in Seattle.

After some initial concern, most PNB board members, exhilarated by the results of their $275,000 gamble, dismissed the City Center incident as of little long-term importance. "Almost all of us felt that was Kent wearing his passion on his sleeve," says chairman Shoup. "The moment it happened and for a while after, it made things difficult for Kent and Francia and the whole company. But it's kind of a legacy now. As time moves on, I think it will be a story told with more approval than disapproval. Kent is soft-spoken and gentle. The fire that burns inside him isn't seen that often. Maybe he needs to have a few more signature acts like that."

But what about Linnette Hitchin, who was all alone on the stage when Kent shouted at Kershaw? What was her response?

"Oh, I was so relieved," she says.

Relieved?!

"When I saw somebody running down the aisle, I thought maybe it was a New York crazy. I was so relieved when I saw it was only Kent."

Kent ponders the next step. Photo by Kurt Smith.

CLASS IX

The Opera House curtain opens on about four dozen girls between six and eight years old dressed in white leotards and pink tights. On their knees in five lines, they create a stage picture that is both dramatic and cute. The audience for the 16th annual performance of the PNB School applauds happily. ❧ The kneeling kids move their arms uniformly, the occasional stray waving arm only heightening their fresh charm. The kids stand up, and together they move their legs in a few basic ballet steps. When they begin jumping, they look like popcorn popping, random but delectable. ❧ As the program continues, ever more advanced students come on stage and perform ever more advanced movements. As the age and accomplishment level of the students proceeds, their turnout gradually increases until the dancers of Level VI, just before intermission, snap effortlessly into snug fifth position. ❧ The production values of the final four pieces are of professional quality, and the dancing is astonishingly good, reflecting both the talent of the young dancers and the expert thoroughness of their training. The Professional Division students' performance of Balanchine's Allegro Brillante *is stunning. The Level VII students in billowing pastel-blue skirts are lovely in Balanchine's* Serenade, *and the advanced students are impressive in* Rapsodia Argentina, *which Kent choreographed especially for them. Then they all get together in a rousing performance of the final portion of Balanchine's* Western Symphony. *Several of the student dancers clearly demonstrate why they were chosen to move on and become apprentices in the PNB company. ❧ Moms, dads, brothers, sisters, grandparents, aunts, uncles and friends are obviously biased, but their applause and shouts of "Bravo!" have an I-didn't-know-they-were-that-good quality. From the second balcony come high-pitched cheers and applause and whistles from the younger students who performed earlier. They clearly have been inspired to become* that *good.*

PACIFIC NORTHWEST BALLET SCHOOL

Francia Russell, Director

Anniversary

TENTH ANNIVERSARY PERFORMANCE   JUNE 15, 1991

"But First a School"

When Lincoln Kirstein, an American eager to have a great ballet company in the United States, met George Balanchine in London in 1933 and asked him if he would come to New York and build such a company, Balanchine reportedly said, "But first a school." Delaying consideration of the PNB School until this chapter is no indication of the school's importance. It is, simply, crucial to the entire PNB organization. More than half of the members of PNB's company had all or part of their training in the school; many students have gone on to pursue professional careers with other dance companies; and who knows how many thousands of former students are now active, supportive ballet enthusiasts who have had their lives significantly affected by the rigorous discipline they learned in the school.

"To my knowledge, there has never been a great ballet company without a great school," says Francia, who is director of the PNB School as well as co–artistic director of the company. When she and Kent came to Seattle in 1977, both taught all day every day, focusing their primary efforts on the school and on doing company-building work before, between and after classes.

Francia: "We're building the future in the school: future dancers, future audiences, future supporters. The school is where the style of the company is shaped. It's our main contact with the community, and it also provides a lot of dancers for productions that we otherwise could not do."

The PNB School is regarded as one of the best in the nation. Its peers, according to Paula Prewett, a former PNB ballet mistress who is now the school's principal, are the School of American Ballet in New York and the San Francisco Ballet School. (Other notable schools include the North Carolina School of the Arts and the schools of the ballet companies in Houston, Boston and Pittsburgh.)

Qualitative judgment of the PNB School is subjective, but its quantitative numbers are specific and impressive. In spring 1997, the school had 630 students, ages 5 to 19, in ten levels, from Pre-Ballet through Professional Division; additionally, 600 adults were enrolled in recreational classes. About two-thirds of the school's 115 classes per week are taught at the Phelps Center, the others at the school's facility in Bellevue. There are six administrative employees, eight full-time and seven part-time teachers, and three full-time pianists plus other part-time accompanists. The school's annual operating budget is $1 million, 70 percent of which is earned and the rest contributed; the earned percentage would be higher, but many promising students are on full or partial scholarships that collectively add up to more than $300,000 per year.

Opposite: PNB School administrator Denise Bolstad in Santa Monica, California, during the 1997 Summer Course audition tour. Photo by Todd Lechtick.

Page 93: Poster for the 1991 PNB School performance.

PNB School's 1992 Creative Movement Tiny Teas performance. Photo by Paul Brown.

Francia: "There are two major strengths that set our school apart. One is that all of our teachers agree on what to teach. This is a result of our continual work on the school's syllabus, which specifies the sequence of steps and exactly how they're taught, with special attention to the musical timing. I don't mean to complain about other ballet schools, but it's very unusual that a ballet school has such consensus among the faculty. And ours is not a rigid consensus, because we regularly talk through everything, and our syllabus is a living, breathing document that's continually refined. The entire faculty participates, but those who have been the most involved in developing the syllabus are Victoria Pulkkinen (the school's curriculum supervisor), Lynne Short, Lisa Peterson, Abbie Siegel, Flemming Halby and Marjorie Thompson. If I had to pick the most dedicated group from all the wonderful people who work at PNB, it would have to be the teachers."

The PNB School's other principal strength, according to Francia, is that it is responsive to the needs of "the total young person." It was the nation's first ballet school to have specialized consultants. Dr. Toby Diamond, a former dancer from New York, is the staff psychologist; Dr. Alan Woodle, the podiatrist; and Peggy Swistak, the nutritionist.

Francia: "We try to work with the whole young dancer, as well as giving the students intellectual stimulation through our seminars on dance history and music and other dance-related topics. We're trying to prepare the students for professional careers. We're very interested in their emotional and intellectual growth as well as their technical dancing skills."

All ballet schools share a problem: too few boys. Among the 630 students in the PNB School in spring 1997, only 70 were boys. This imbalance results, of course, from the public attitude that ballet is suitable and indeed desirable for girls but boys ought to be out playing sports. Boys generally get along well as ballet students until age 12 or 13, when peer pressure causes many pubescent boys to quit dancing. Ballet schools cannot by themselves alter this situation; only a societal change in attitude toward ballet can do that.

Kent: "The perception that ballet is gay won't change until homophobia disappears. American culture is pretty severe. We carry guns and shoot people. I don't know that a kinder, gentler America is going to happen soon. The homophobic reaction to ballet doesn't exist in Europe—maybe in England, but not on the Continent."

The PNB School's summer course is prized among young dancers throughout the nation. In spring 1997, 1,600 young dancers in 21 cities auditioned for the course; 125 were chosen to join with 100 local students to participate in the six-week course at the Phelps Center.

"When I planned our first audition trip in 1980, Francia went alone to six cities," recalls Denise Bolstad, the school administrator. "I practically begged other schools to let us use their facilities for the auditions. And could they please pick up Francia at the airport? And did someone have an extra bed where Francia could sleep? Now the other schools are begging *us* to come, and several of us go on our annual audition tours, which are set up very professionally. And we get lots of calls from parents all over the country, asking for advice on their child's ballet career."

Paula Prewett: "The most promising dancers accepted for the summer course are given full scholarship, housing and a stipend. Our audition trips are not unlike football recruiting. We go around the country seeking the best talent. The competition for the best young dancers is very tough now."

Denise Bolstad: "All the top schools are auditioning and vying for the same kids. In the early years, we'd select students from auditions, call them with our acceptance, and they'd turn us down to go to other schools. That doesn't happen much anymore."

Paula Prewett: "I admire the young dancers, and I'm in awe of what the parents do. Studying ballet involves a big investment of money and time. We insist on reliable, prompt attendance at class; parents have to see to it that our schedule is met. The students love to dance, and they get so much from it in terms of focus, discipline and working toward goals. It's not unusual for former students who have achieved success in professions other than dance to come back and tell us that they credit their ballet training for their success."

For some students, the school provides the foundation for a career in dance. It also functions as a feeder system for PNB's performing company; four Professional Division dancers were chosen in spring 1997 to become apprentices with the company. Six more Professional Division dancers were selected for apprenticeship with other American ballet companies.

Francia: "We help our students prepare their resumés, get good photos and make travel arrangements for their tours to audition for other companies. A lot of counseling goes into this process. One of our new trustees gave a very enlightened grant to provide the students with financial support for their audition tours."

The school demands hard work from students who want to continue through the levels of achievement and instruction. The school also exacts long hours and concentrated work from its faculty and staff. Anyone with even a hint of doubt about the school's worth and its results should attend an annual school performance at the end of the school

Francia with PNB School principal Paula Prewett.

DanceChance students in the PNB School's annual performance. Photo by Joann Arruda.

Opposite: Linnette Hitchin and Paul Gibson perform in Kent's Quaternary *during a Bravo! Ballet performance.* Photo by Kurt Smith.

year in June. While the little kids are cute, they also are clearly disciplined. And the older students? They're simply breathtaking.

Francia: "Our job is to help prepare the students for life, through the discipline and beauty of dance. The core philosophy of the school is to demand of each student, whether or not a dance career is planned, the very best effort of which he or she is capable, and to give in return the care and attention the student deserves."

Included among the school's students—and performing together in the annual school performances—are youngsters in PNB's DanceChance program. These students are introduced to ballet in twice-a-week classes during the regular school day, and those who are talented and motivated are supported for further training in the school. In 1994, DanceChance had four partner schools. In the 1996–97 school year, 12 Seattle schools were involved; 663 third-graders were screened, and 65 were invited to the six-week introductory classes. In 1996–97, six youngsters from the 1994 pilot program were in the school's Level III; additionally, there were 10 second-year and 31 first-year students.

DanceChance is supported by numerous individuals, foundations and governmental agencies. When funding is sufficient, there are plans to expand the program to schools on the Eastside and throughout King County.

Bravo! Ballet, a PNB outreach program started in 1992, is designed to teach fourth-through eighth-grade students—and their teachers—about ballet by having PNB teachers conduct classes at the schools, by bringing students to the Phelps Center to take a class and then to observe PNB company members in class or rehearsal, and by presenting Opera House performances designed especially for the students. Bravo! Ballet is administered by Jeanie Thomas, who since 1990 has served as PNB's resident scholar and research expert as well as its director of education. The program is supported by PNB, grants and donations, and modest fees.

"Teachers are the key," says Thomas. "We are experts in ballet, but they are experts in teaching. We put the two talents together." This connection includes study guides to help the teachers prepare the students for performances and classes, free workshops for the teachers, students' field trips to the Phelps Center, in-school instruction and residencies, and the special performances at the Opera House. During its five-year history, Bravo! Ballet has introduced more than 25,000 students to ballet.

CLASS X

Late afternoon sunlight blazes through the floor-to-ceiling windows in Studio C. Dancers move in and out of slashes of sunlight as they perform Balanchine's Mozartiana *for an invited audience seated in the studio balcony and in two rows of chairs on three sides of the studio. This is one of the workshop rehearsals that take place several days before every PNB opening night. ❦ The dancers are in rehearsal garb, some neat, some grubby. They are without the sets, costumes, makeup and lights they will have on opening night, but their presence is more immediate. Often the dancers come within inches of spectators in the front rows, and when they leap "off stage," it seems inevitable that one of them will land in a spectator's lap. But they don't. ❦ With unconcealed joy and never entirely hidden effort, they perform Glen Tetley's lyrical* Voluntaries, *in which difficult acrobatic movements flow together in stunning beauty. The dancers have no theatrical artifice to hide behind. They are the dance itself. They clearly love it, enjoying their hyper-physical artistry and the contrast between their airy mobility and the open-mouthed appreciation of the sedentary audience. The dancers' perspiration, rarely visible in the Opera House, now flashes golden as they move through the patches of sunlight. ❦ The workshop ends with Val Caniparoli's* Lambarena, *a vigorous ballet set to a melding of the music of Bach and traditional African music. The work demands that the dancers go all out, and their energy holds the audience transfixed, even when twirling dancers spin beads of perspiration over the audience. ❦ At the end of* Lambarena, *the 200 or so onlookers applaud and cheer and then applaud and cheer some more. Francia moves to the center of the studio and tells the audience: "There's not a single classical ballet step in what you've just seen. This shows that well-trained ballet dancers can dance* anything!"

Prejudice
and Pride

A common idea about ballet dancers is that they, like nuns and monks, lead lives of pure devotion and dedication, isolated from the "real world" (whatever that is) by the unrelenting discipline essential for the aesthetic (and ascetic) life in the world of ballet. There is some truth in that, but it ignores the fact that most ballet dancers are in their teens and 20s and are physically super-fit, with all of the raging hormones that are both the joy and the curse of the young and healthy. An even more common notion is that all male ballet dancers are gay. That assumption was deftly skewered by Otto Neubert, PNB's German-born ballet master, at a PNB dinner. He and his stunning female companion, Ariana Lallone, a principal dancer in the PNB company, were seated next to a macho corporate executive who, in a challenging tone, asked Neubert: "How many homosexuals are there in the PNB company?" Neubert replied quickly: "Probably about the same percentage as in your company."

Neubert's droll humor works in happy counterpoint to the intensity of rehearsal and performance. In April 1997, he was seated in the back row of the Opera House to observe the American debut of the company's newest member, Batkhurel Bold, a tall, muscular dancer who was born in Ulan Bator, Mongolia, and trained in Perm, Russia. As the house lights dimmed for *Western Symphony,* a Balanchine ballet in which the dancers portray dance-hall girls and cowboys, Neubert whispered to his seatmate: "This is a funny ballet." The seatmate nodded in agreement and Neubert continued: "If you think the ballet is funny, you should have seen a *German* trying to teach a *Mongolian* how to be an *American* cowboy."

Other dancers in PNB's 50-member company come from France, Belgium, Japan, Canada, Siberia, Estonia, Russia, Holland and Albania, as well as from 17 U.S. states plus the District of Columbia and Puerto Rico. Training, hard work, discipline, close cooperation—all are part of a dancer's life, and many share the attitude expressed by Anne Derieux, a native of France and a PNB principal dancer: "When I come to rehearsal every day and I know that I'm going to learn something new that will help me improve my dancing, I'm happy. I don't ask for anything more. The day it would not be like this is the day I stop dancing."

Some dancers stop because they have to. Injuries can sideline even the best and fittest of them. To create their art, dancers must continually push their bodies to their physical limits every day, all day, every week, all week. And fear of injury, even a career-ending injury, is always near the surface of a dancer's consciousness.

Still, dancers tough it out. Anyone who thinks ballet is for delicate, namby-pamby wisps doesn't know his namby from his pamby. Ballet dancers, men and women, are

Opposite: Anne Derieux in Glen Tetley's Voluntaries. Photo by Kurt Smith.

Page 101: Ariana Lallone and Konstantin Kouzin rehearse Lambarena *with choreographer Val Caniparoli. PNB ballet master Otto Neubert looks on.* Photo by Kurt Smith.

In a publicity photo, Paul Gibson soars as Oberon in Balanchine's A Midsummer Night's Dream. *An injury prevented his performing the role.* Photo by Ben Kerns.

among the strongest, most agile and most highly trained athletes in the world. If you think ballet is easy, just try a couple of the basic foot positions. Hold your heels together and turn your toes out so they're pointing in opposite directions. That's first position. Still stable? Now, keeping both feet pointing away from each other, snug your right foot behind and up against your left foot. That's fifth position. What? You can't do it?

Paul Gibson, a PNB principal dancer since October 1995, knows that an ankle or foot injury can also cause pain in the heart. In October 1996, as the company was rehearsing for its New York engagement, Gibson came down from a jump and his foot "just gave out." He recalls: "I didn't do the jump wrong. I didn't come down wrong. My ankle just said, 'Okay, this is it!' " Gibson not only could not dance with the company in New York, but was out for 14 weeks. Then in June 1997, during the dress rehearsal for *A Midsummer Night's Dream*, in which he was dancing the principal role of Oberon, Gibson felt pain in his foot during the first act. He finished the first and second acts, dancing through pain. When he went to the doctor the next day, he learned that he had a broken bone in his foot. No *Midsummer*. Out seven weeks.

The pleasure that is the flip side of pain is more difficult to isolate and express, but it is no less real for being intangible. You can see it in a dancer's face, a confident smile that is different from the pasted-on smiles of chorus lines. You can see it in a dancer's body language, buoyant and assured. Dancers feel pleasure and give pleasure. As Balanchine said of ballet: "First of all, it is a pleasure."

Over its first quarter century, PNB has given pleasure to hundreds of thousands. That achievement is the result of the talent and commitment of many hundreds of dancers and support staff. It's impossible to list all those who have been with PNB through its painful times and rewarding times, but it's necessary to single out a few.

Randall G. (Rico) Chiarelli started with PNB in 1979 as resident lighting designer and technical director. Son of the architect of the Seattle Opera House, Chiarelli is genetical-

Kent speaks to dancers in rehearsal of his Cinderella. *Ballet master Otto Neubert and pianist Dianne Chilgren look on.* Photo by Jill Sabella.

Larae Hascall and PNB School student Blaire Pawluk

preparing for PNB's Nutcracker. PNB photo.

Opposite: Patricia Barker putting on her pointe shoes.

Photo by Kurt Smith.

ly programmed for life in the theatre. The company relies on his unflappable expertise in stagecraft. His quick wit rewards the deserving and deflates the pretentious. His crew's competence and can-do attitude have earned them the respect of the company and the nickname "Five Neat Guys."

Patricia Barker is the veteran of the company, and although PNB is by design a company without stars, she has that special something that causes audiences and critics to regard her as a genuine star. A scholarship student in the PNB School, she was taken into the company as an apprentice in 1980 and became a full member in 1981, a soloist in 1984 and a principal in 1986. Not only is she blessed with great talent, but she also has extraordinary strength and the gutsy willingness to take the risks that create electrifying performances.

Deborah Hadley and Benjamin Houk are gifted dancers who were PNB stalwarts for many seasons. As individuals, their dancing was precise, beautiful and exciting. Together they created the kind of chemistry that illuminated the stage and entranced audiences. The most notable example of their dancing was in *The Tragedy of Romeo and Juliet*, which Kent choreographed especially for them and which stands as one of the highest achievements in PNB's history. Houk is now artistic director of the Nashville Ballet.

Rebecca Wakefield retired as production stage manager in June 1997 after 16 years with the company. From the wings, she called many hundreds of performances for PNB at the Opera House and on tour. A skilled professional, she also served the company well by calming nerves and deftly puncturing pomposity.

Stewart Kershaw has been PNB's music director/conductor since 1983. In the mid-1980s, he played a crucial part in developing PNB's own fully professional orchestra, which gave the company a musical continuity and integrity it had previously not had. A widely experienced conductor of orchestral music as well as ballet music, he is also the founder and conductor of the Auburn Symphony Orchestra in suburban Seattle.

Allan Dameron was recruited by Kershaw to become PNB's associate conductor. An excellent pianist as well as an accomplished conductor, Dameron is esteemed highly for his superb musicianship and diligence.

Dianne Chilgren, who for many years was Balanchine's rehearsal pianist, would be a treasure in any ballet company. She is, says Francia, "my good right hand. She knows more about ballet than anyone."

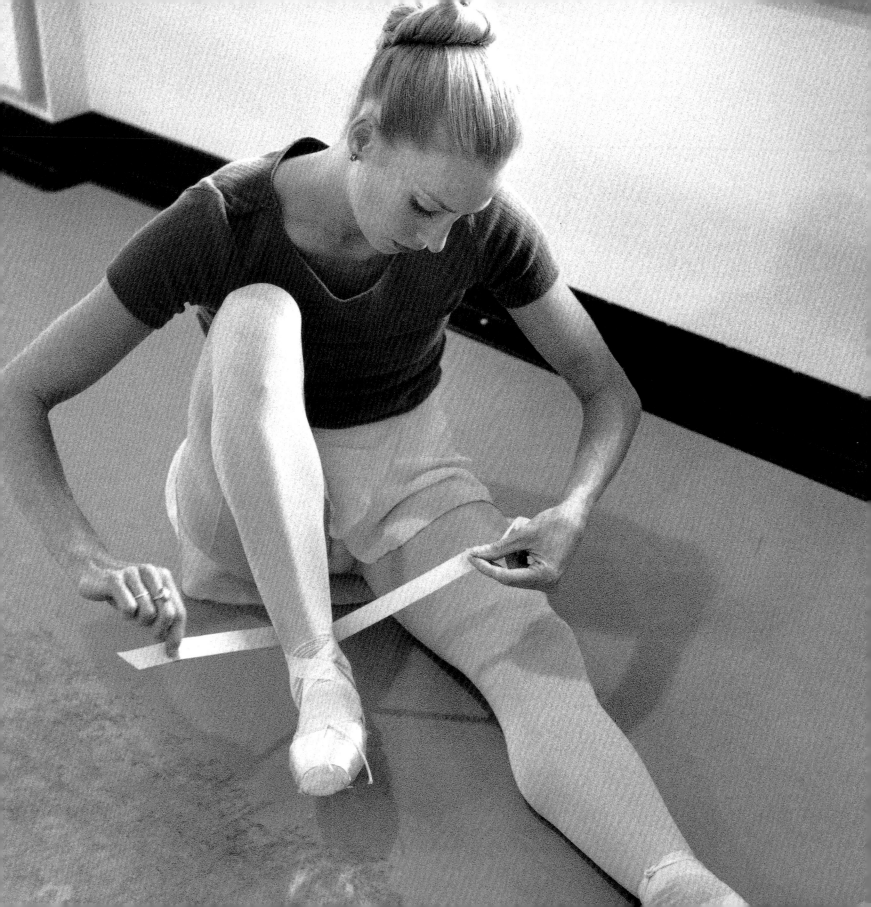

Ballet mistress Lisa McCallister talks with PNB School

students before a Nutcracker *performance.*

Photo by Kurt Smith.

Larae Theige Hascall has worked in PNB's costume shop since 1983 and been its manager since 1987. She regularly makes the impossible possible. During the creation of the new production of *A Midsummer Night's Dream*, her shop turned out all of the show's props and 120 new costumes, many of them exquisitely detailed (and at an average cost of $2,000 each!). In the frenzied final days before opening night, she supervised a team of more than 70 artisans.

John Pendleton, PNB's company manager, wears many hats, and prominent among them is tour arranger. Experienced in arts presentation (he worked with such famed companies as the Metropolitan Opera and the Bolshoi Ballet), he has set up PNB's major tours and juggled their multitudinous details. He has developed extensive connections in the Far East that could lead to a PNB tour there in the near future. He's also exploring touring to major festivals in Holland, Seoul and Edinburgh.

Lisa McCallister, PNB's retiring ballet mistress, was the subject of a poignant tribute at a company party after the final performance of the 1996–97 season. As company retirees were being presented with gifts and subjected to good-natured roasting, the mood was one of collegial joviality. When it was McCallister's turn to be honored, Kent took the microphone, but he was unable to speak. Choked with emotion, he bit his lip and dropped his head as he attempted to regain his composure. In a room that had rocked with raucous laughter only moments before, it suddenly became so quiet that you could almost hear the tears welling up in many eyes. Finally Kent spoke a bit haltingly but eloquently about McCallister's invaluable contributions to him and to the company over many years. Then he and McCallister hugged each other for a long time to a crescendo of applause and cheers.

An ovation is also due Sheffield Phelps and all the men and women who have worked diligently and selflessly as PNB chairmen and presidents. Cheers seem inadequate for Kent and Francia. "*They* are the story of PNB," says Susan Brotman, chair of the PNB board from 1992 to 1996, expressing a unanimous opinion.

Kent and Francia are quick to return the compliment: "When she was chair, Susan worked shoulder to shoulder with us during a time of great change for PNB. She came to the Phelps Center daily and worked with clear focus and great efficiency. We will always be grateful for all she has done, and is doing, for PNB."

Before Kent and Francia accepted the 1988 Washington State Governor's Arts Award, each prepared a thank-you speech for the award ceremony. Without ever discussing what the other was going to say, both expressed gratitude to the entire PNB family and then ended their brief speeches by expressing their thanks to those they felt were most important: their three sons.

Their oldest son, Christopher, joined the San Francisco Ballet 12 years ago and has been a principal dancer in that company for eight years. Their middle son, Darren, is involved in sports marketing in Seattle. Their youngest son, Ethan, is a chef at The Ruins, a private club in Seattle.

Francia: "The ones who made it possible for us to do our work, who have been tolerant and kept us sane, are our sons. Our three sons are our *real* accomplishment."

Kent: "The rewards of our sons growing up to become terrific young men are greater than any accolades we could ever get out of the ballet."

Later Kent and Francia extended their expressions of gratitude: "We came here originally because Shef Phelps and Jerry Sanford promised that the PNB board would support us in building a major company and a school of equal importance. The board has stuck with that promise through thick and thin for 20 years. The big reward we've had in working in Seattle and with all the progress PNB has made is the opportunity we've had to work with an amazing group of people—the dancers, the musicians, the administrative staff, the production and artistic staff, wardrobe, the crew, the school's faculty, the board, community leaders and volunteers. We've had the good fortune to work with an incredible number of dedicated and talented people to make a ballet company happen."

Kent and Francia with their son Christopher at the

Dance Magazine Awards in New York.

CLASS XI

With apologies to King Solomon: For, lo, the preparation is past, the rehearsals are over and gone; the dancers appear on the stage; the time of opening night is come, and the sound of *merde* is heard in the theatre. ❦ *The expletive, milder in French than in its English translation, is ballet's traditional expression of good luck, the equivalent of the theatre's "break a leg." The Opera House's bulletin boards display good-luck messages from friends, relatives and other supporters, all wishing the dancers "many merdes." ❦ Just out of view off stage right, Rebecca Wakefield, the production stage manager, wearing a headset with microphone, calls: "Places, everyone." The dancers quickly comply. Moments later, applause greets conductor Stewart Kershaw, who suddenly becomes visible on one of the two television screens behind Rebecca. The orchestra begins playing. Rebecca says, "Curtain, go!" and two hefty stagehands pull on the rope that raises the heavy red velvet curtain. The posed dancers begin to move. The show has begun. The audience view of the stage appears on the other TV screen. ❦ The performance goes smoothly. One of the female dancers makes a slight misstep that's probably unnoticed by the audience. She continues dancing easily, smiling all the while, but when she comes off stage, she barks out the English equivalent of* merde. ❦ *A male dancer is now performing a demanding solo. He makes the leaps and turns look easy. After he exits to applause, he stops just off stage, bends over, puts his hands on his knees and gasps for air. ❦ From the wings, the women appear light and delicate, almost ethereal. When they come off stage, they are dotted with perspiration. Their heads drop, their shoulders slump and, with their feet still turned out as they walk, they incongruously waddle like ducks.*

Living on the Edge

11

CHAPTER

"Transplanting ballet in this country is like trying to raise a palm tree in Dakota," Lincoln Kirstein said in a moment of frustration during his and Balanchine's cultivation of the New York City Ballet. Although more moist and verdant than the Dakotas, Washington State seemed for many years an unlikely place for a ballet company to take root. The Evergreen State was noted for its many talented dancers and choreographers who would come and go—mostly go. But now Pacific Northwest Ballet has survived in Seattle long enough to put down deep roots and send forth silver blossoms for its 25th-anniversary season.

To shift the metaphor, PNB is one of many Seattle arts organizations lifted by the tide of rising artistic interest in a metropolitan area of high-tech industry, high educational achievement and high lifestyle expectations. The pop world may know Seattle for grunge music, Boeing airplanes, Microsoft software and Starbucks coffee, but the city also is increasingly the object of national and international attention as an arts hot spot. During PNB's 1996 Kennedy Center engagement, Francia told the *Washington Times*: "We're lucky because we arrived in Seattle at the right time, when Seattle was just beginning to grow, and we've taken off together."

Peter Donnelly, president of the Seattle-based Corporate Council for the Arts, which over the years has supported PNB to the tune of $1.7 million, comments: "Everyone in the arts community likes Kent and Francia, likes them as people who succeed at their work and also function as part of the larger community. PNB is financially very solid, and it knows its responsibilities. The three legs of its stool—fiscal, artistic, board—are all very strong now. Moreover, nobody's talking about a limited financial pie here anymore. Between the construction of the Bagley Wright Theatre [for the Seattle Repertory Theatre] in 1983 and the opening of Benaroya Hall [for the Seattle Symphony] in the 1998–99 season, the community will have spent $404 million in capital building programs for the arts."

Donnelly is correct in noting that PNB's public image is one of success, especially after its New York triumph in October 1996, but it can be argued that the company is in danger of becoming a victim of its own success. Because the organization has always paid its own way, diligently avoiding red-ink seasons, it has never had the pleading fund drives that are common in the nonprofit arts community; unlike many other arts groups, PNB has never had to throw itself on the mercy of the public and beg for money to insure its survival. Even the arts-savvy public may think PNB is crying wolf when it says it has urgent needs to increase its endowment, to finance much-needed capital construction and to balance its books during the next few seasons. PNB has consistently earned an

Opposite: Ariana Lallone in Caniparoli's Lambarena.
Photo by Ben Kerns.

Page 111: Kabby Mitchell in Kent's Over the Waves.
PNB photo.

PNB president David F. Hill with Susan Brotman, who served four years as PNB chair.

amazing 70 percent of its annual income at the box office; the other 30 percent comes from contributions and grants. But the company has run out of ways to increase its box-office earnings. And if PNB doesn't continue to grow, it will surely begin to wither. The reason for the earnings block is simple: until the Seattle Symphony moves into its new concert hall, PNB cannot get additional performance dates in the Opera House, and without more performances, PNB can't increase its income without prohibitive hikes in ticket prices.

"We're looking at deficit financing for several years," says David F. Hill, PNB's president. "We have cash reserves now of over a million dollars, but we need to make an investment for the future. We have had many spirited debates over deficits. The New York tour is one example, but look at the results of that. We have realized that we're going to go through a revenue valley for several years. However, if we are the vibrant, successful organization I think we are, we're going to climb out of that. I think our opportunities for income will increase in the future with more performances in the Opera House and with a successful endowment campaign that will alleviate some of the pressure for income. What I'm concerned about is that you can get addicted to deficit spending, and clearly that's not good. The success of PNB over the long term has been that it adhered strictly, year in and year out, to the idea of maintaining a balanced budget. In the next few years, we're going to have to wean ourselves off of that. There's always a way to find more money if you think you have to. We are going to maintain very strict discipline."

In addition to the endowment campaign headed by former PNB chair Susan Brotman, the organization is seeking capital funds to build a new facility for the PNB School on the Eastside and to acquire and remodel the exhibition area beneath the Phelps Center to meet the pressing need for expansion experienced by both the school and the company. PNB is also deeply involved in an Opera House remodeling that is projected to occur before the year 2000; it will update the structure, last renovated in 1962, and make significant changes to improve it as a theatre for dance.

Chairman Shoup adds to the list: "We're also talking about more touring, enlarging the company from 50 dancers to 65, enhancing the benefits we provide to the dancers, bringing more great teachers here, attracting more great talent from around the world. We're talking about all those things. I think everyone would agree that Kent will never be satisfied, will always have a bigger vision. I think that's great! The organization is very fortunate to have both Kent and Francia—Francia with her feet on the ground, worrying about how we're going to get through the day, and Kent the visionary saying, 'Forget about the day, let's dream about the future.' If someone 25 years ago had listed the top metropolitan areas in the United States and then asked which of those cities would have one of the nation's top three or four ballet companies in 25 years, Seattle certainly would not have made anyone's list of the top ten. What has been accomplished here is miraculous. Certainly it all starts with Kent and Francia and their absolute commitment to constant improvement, their constant commitment to world-class standards and their ability to sell that vision to others. Not only are Kent and Francia yin and yang, but on any given day they can probably decide who's yin and who's yang on that day."

Francia and Kent with PNB chairman Allen C. Shoup.

Ballet is a feast for the eyes and ears and an energizing stimulant for the mind and spirit. It can be rollicking fun or a tissue-soaker, stark or lush, a frenzy of action or a dream of lyricism. Other performing arts, especially classical music and opera, rely heavily on works created in the 18th and 19th centuries, and their basic function, while undoubtedly important, is that of a museum. Ballet, on the other hand, constantly renews itself with new works, living vibrantly on the edge of contemporary life. To be sure, ballet companies still present 19th-century works like *Swan Lake* and *The Nutcracker,* but the great majority of most ballet companies' repertoire—and this is definitely true for PNB—are works of the 20th century, and many are works that were created last year, last month, last week, yesterday.

Allen Shoup says: "I think that ballet might be the art form for the 21st century. In our current high-tech society, we are exposed to so many stimuli that it takes more now to capture our attention. Ballet floods the senses more completely than other art forms. Movement, music, color, design, theatricality: ballet has so many different aspects that it probably serves better to entertain and enhance the senses than other art forms today. If people don't realize that, it's only because they haven't been exposed to it."

If Shoup did not exist, it would be necessary for Kent the visionary to invent him.

Shoup continues: "One of the problems PNB has is that it came so far so quickly that many of its most committed supporters, including many board members, are people who remember that they literally had to pick up hammers and nails and help build sets, sweep up the floors and go out and hand-sell tickets. They were truly critical parts of the staff of the organization. Now that PNB has grown and become successful, the board has hired very competent staff and has evolved into doing what a true board is supposed to do: not the day-in-day-out business but delegating and sitting as a kind of oversight committee. That situation creates frustration among some members of the board because they think they should be doing more, because they used to do more."

The whole PNB family is now facing challenges that would intimidate even the bravest heart: preparing, promoting, presenting and paying for a 25th-anniversary season that consists of a gala retrospective season-opener followed by ten world premieres and four Seattle premieres. The season chosen by Kent and Francia makes a strong statement about PNB's pride in its past, its confidence in its present and its hopes for the future. It's surely a mega-challenge for everyone in PNB: for the dancers, who have 14 new works to learn and perform; for the production staff, whose work increases exponentially with multiple premieres; for the administration, which also has a heavier work load and, moreover, is charged with selling a season that has no proven hits and a group of relatively unknown choreographers; and for the board, which has to figure out how to pay for all of it. Among all the uncertainties of the silver-anniversary season, there are several sure things: everyone in PNB will be pushed to the limit, no one will have a second of yawning boredom, and it will be a season that none of the participants will ever forget.

Beyond the anniversary season, the challenges PNB is facing are abundant and formidable. But since Kent and Francia arrived in Seattle in 1977, PNB has always been challenged, has always taken risks, has always lived on the edge. Kent and Francia have not simply pushed the envelope. They have created a whole new envelope.

"Working with Kent and Francia is a treat," says Susan Brotman. "I have great respect for them and for their careers, and also for the kind of operation they have built and the kind of people they select to work with. They have very high levels of expertise and expectation. They bring out the best in everyone. In working with them, you want to be as good at what you do as they are at what they do."

Let's go on.

Francia and Kent rehearse for the first Nutcracker Ball in 1989. PNB photo.

Opposite: PNB's 1996 production of Carmina Burana. Photo by David Cooper.

Ballet Name	Choreographer	Composer	Seattle Premiere
Agam	Kent Stowell	Gerhard Samuel	February 1983
Agon	George Balanchine	Igor Stravinsky	March 1993
Alice	Glen Tetley	David del Tredici	February 1992
Allegro Brillante	George Balanchine	Peter Ilyich Tchaikovsky	March 1979
Amazed in Burning Dreams	Kirk Peterson	Philip Glass	November 1993
American Gesture	Lar Lubovitch	Charles Ives	February 1992
Anima Mundi	Kent Stowell	Richard Danielpour	April 1996
Apollo	George Balanchine	Igor Stravinsky	February 1993
Artifact Part II	William Forsythe	Johann Sebastian Bach	February 1998
Ballet Imperial	George Balanchine	Peter Ilyich Tchaikovsky	November 1997
Black Iris	Lynn Dally	Duke Ellington	February 1984
Bournonville Variations	August Bournonville	Edvard Helsted/ Holger Simon Paulli	February 1988
Brahms-Schoenberg Quartet	George Balanchine	Johannes Brahms/ Arnold Schoenberg	February 1985
Brandenburg Concerti	Ib Andersen	Johann Sebastian Bach	February 1994
By When	Benjamin Houk	Georg Muffat	April 1989
Cage, The	Jerome Robbins	Igor Stravinsky	October 1984
Carmina Burana	Kent Stowell	Carl Orff	October 1993
Cascade	Lucinda Childs	Steve Reich	March 1984
Chaconne	George Balanchine	Christoph Willibald von Gluck	February 1984
Chrysalis Regarding	Clark Tippet	John Adams	October 1990
Cinderella	Kent Stowell	Sergei Prokofiev	May 1994
Cinderella	Ben Stevenson	Sergei Prokofiev	May 1980
Clarion	Lucinda Childs	Paul Chihara	May 1986
Company B	Paul Taylor	Andrews Sisters	February 1993
Con Amore	Lew Christensen	Gioacchino Rossini	November 1986
Concerto Barocco	George Balanchine	Johann Sebastian Bach	April 1978
Concerto Grosso	Charles Czarny	George Frideric Handel	April 1980
Coppélia	Kent Stowell	Léo Delibes	June 1978
Daphnis and Chloe	Kent Stowell	Maurice Ravel	February 1979
Dark Elegies	Antony Tudor	Gustav Mahler	March 1987
Delicate Balance	Kent Stowell	Frédéric Chopin	February 1988
Deranged Dances	Kent Stowell	Charles Ives	February 1980
Diversions	Paul Gibson	Morton Gould	April 1998
Divertimento No. 15	George Balanchine	Wolfgang Amadeus Mozart	February 1991
Dumbarton Oaks	Kent Stowell	Igor Stravinsky	February 1982
Duo Fantasy	Kent Stowell	William Bolcom	March 1989
Fanfare	Jerome Robbins	Benjamin Britten	November 1994
Fauré Requiem	Kent Stowell	Gabriel Fauré	March 1993
Filling Station	Lew Christensen	Virgil Thomson	September 1978
Firebird	Kent Stowell	Igor Stravinsky	May 1990
Four Temperaments, The	George Balanchine	Paul Hindemith	February 1978
Gigue	Clark Tippet	Johann Sebastian Bach	April 1990
Ginastera	Rudi van Dantzig	Alberto Ginastera	January 1998
Gran Partita	Val Caniparoli	Wolfgang Amadeus Mozart	March 1991
Hail to the Conquering Hero	Kent Stowell	George Frideric Handel	October 1985
Harlequinade Pas de Deux	George Balanchine	Riccardo Drigo	November 1982

Ballet Name	Choreographer	Composer	Seattle Premiere
Harp Concerto Pas de Deux	Michael Smuin	Carl Reinecke	April 1980
Il Distratto	Lew Christensen	Franz Joseph Haydn	May 1980
Jardí Tancat	Nacho Duato	Maria del Mar Bonet	February 1996
Jardin aux Lilas	Antony Tudor	Ernest Chausson	November 1987
Kammer-Garten Tänze	Kent Stowell	Wolfgang Amadeus Mozart	March 1991
Karelia	Kent Stowell	Jean Sibelius	September 1978
L'Heure Bleue	Kent Stowell	Maurice Ravel	April 1978
La Bergère Celimene	Kent Stowell	Wolfgang Amadeus Mozart	February 1985
La Valse	George Balanchine	Maurice Ravel	May 1981
La Ventana Pas de Trois	August Bournonville	Hans Christian Lumbye	February 1979
Lambarena	Val Caniparoli	Johann Sebastian Bach and traditional African	April 1997
Le Jazz	Bill Evans	Bohuslav Martinů	March 1981
Lento, a Tempo, e Appassionato	Vincente Nebrada	Alexander Scriabin	May 1982
Les Biches	Mark Dendy	Francis Poulenc	March 1997
Les Cerises Perdues	Margo Sappington	George Gershwin	May 1981
Light Years	Pat Graney	Arvo Pärt	November 1988
Lone Poems	Loyce Houlton	Ralph Vaughn Williams	May 1980
Madrigalesco	Benjamin Harkarvy	Antonio Vivaldi	April 1980
Matrix	Ian Horvath	Béla Bartók	February 1987
Mercury	Lynne Taylor-Corbett	Franz Joseph Haydn	February 1995
Midsummer Night's Dream, A	George Balanchine	Felix Mendelssohn	May 1985
Moor's Pavane, The	José Limón	Henry Purcell	November 1986
Mozartiana	George Balanchine	Peter Ilyich Tchaikovsky	November 1994
New Coburn Bruning	Diane Coburn Bruning	Igor Stravinsky	November 1997
New Donald Byrd	Donald Byrd	William Bolcom	January 1998
New Kevin O'Day	Kevin O'Day	Graham Fitkin	November 1997
New Lynn Dally	Lynn Dally	Thelonius Monk, arranged by Norman Durkee	January 1998
New Mark Dendy	Mark Dendy	Philip Glass	February 1998
New Val Caniparoli	Val Caniparoli	Dmitri Shostakovich	April 1998
No. 1 Sweet Levinsky	Hugh Bigney	Paul Hindemith	April 1989
Nutcracker, The	Kent Stowell	Peter Ilyich Tchaikovsky	December 1983
Octet	Marjorie Mussman	Igor Stravinsky	March 1982
Orpheus Portrait	Kent Stowell	Franz Liszt	February 1990
Over the Waves	Kent Stowell	G. Hubbard Miller	April 1978
Pacing	Miriam Mahdaviani	Steve Reich	February 1998
Painting the London Bridge	Lucinda Hughey	Walter Piston	April 1989
Paquita	Marius Petipa	Léon (or Louis) Minkus	May 1990
Pas de Deux Campagnolo	Kent Stowell	Giuseppe Verdi	May 1981
Poème Saint-Saëns	Kent Stowell	Camille Saint-Saëns	November 1990
Prodigal Son	George Balanchine	Sergei Prokofiev	April 1984
Quaternary	Kent Stowell	Sergei Rachmaninoff	March 1995
Quilt, The	Lynne Taylor-Corbett	Benjamin Britten	April 1996
Ragtime	Kent Stowell	Igor Stravinsky	February 1978
Ramifications	Rudi van Dantzig	György Ligeti, Henry Purcell	February 1991
Rapture	Lila York	Sergei Prokofiev	April 1996
Rassemblement	Nacho Duato	Toto Bissainthe	April 1998

BALLET NAME	CHOREOGRAPHER	COMPOSER	SEATTLE PREMIERE
Ravel Concerto	John Clifford	Maurice Ravel	February 1986
Ravenna	Kent Stowell	Gioacchino Rossini	April 1984
Romeo and Juliet Pas de Deux	Kent Stowell	Sergei Prokofiev	April 1984
Roses	Paul Taylor	Richard Wagner/Heinrich Baermann	April 1988
Rubies	George Balanchine	Igor Stravinsky	February 1988
Salute	Bruce Wells	Igor Stravinsky	May 1982
Satie	John Clifford	Erik Satie	April 1987
Seattle Slew	Kent Stowell	William Bolcom	March 1986
Septet	Merce Cunningham	Erik Satie	November 1989
Serenade	George Balanchine	Peter Ilyich Tchaikovsky	September 1978
Shostakovich Piano Concerto	Jean-Paul Comelin	Dmitri Shostakovich	February 1980
Silver Lining	Kent Stowell	Jerome Kern	May 1998
Sinfonia Concertante	Lar Lubovitch	Wolfgang Amadeus Mozart	February 1991
Six Waltzes	Vincente Nebrada	Sergei Prokofiev	April 1983
Sondheim Suite	Ann Reinking, William Whitener	Stephen Sondheim	November 1989
Songs of Mahler	Michael Smuin	Gustav Mahler	February 1982
Souvenirs	Todd Bolender	Samuel Barber	April 1984
Square Dance	George Balanchine	Archangelo Corelli/ Antonio Vivaldi	March 1981
Stars and Stripes	George Balanchine	John Philip Sousa/Hershy Kay	March 1983
Stravinsky Piano Pieces	Michael Smuin	Igor Stravinsky	October 1984
Street Songs	Val Caniparoli	Carl Orff	July 1980
Swan Lake	Kent Stowell	Peter Ilyich Tchaikovsky	April 1981
Sylvia Pas de Deux	André Eglevsky after Balanchine	Léo Delibes	November 1987
Symmetries	Mark Dendy	John Adams	February 1994
Symphonic Impressions	Kent Stowell	Igor Stravinsky	September 1978
Symphony in C	George Balanchine	Georges Bizet	March 1987
Symphony No. 5	Kent Stowell	Franz Schubert	February 1978
Tarantella Pas de Deux	George Balanchine	Louis Moreau Gottschalk	January 1985
Tchaikovsky Pas de Deux	George Balanchine	Peter Ilyich Tchaikovsky	August 1985
Tenderness of Patient Minds, The	Ton Simons	Wolfgang Amadeus Mozart	November 1996
Terre à Terre	Ian Horvath	Peter Ilyich Tchaikovsky	April 1985
Theme and Variations	George Balanchine	Peter Ilyich Tchaikovsky	October 1985
Three Epitaphs	Paul Taylor	American Folk Music	February 1989
Through Interior Worlds	Kent Stowell	Joseph Schwantner	October 1992
Time and Ebb	Kent Stowell	Sergei Prokofiev	November 1991
Tragedy of Romeo and Juliet, The	Kent Stowell	Peter Ilyich Tchaikovsky	June 1987
Tunes	Lynne Taylor-Corbett	Charles Strouse	November 1991
Valse Fantaisie	George Balanchine	Mikhail Glinka	February 1992
Variations Serieuses	Choo San Goh	Felix Mendelssohn	May 1978
Violin Concerto	George Balanchine	Igor Stravinsky	March 1986
Voluntaries	Glen Tetley	Francis Poulenc	February 1990
Western Symphony	George Balanchine	Hershy Kay	February 1982
Who Cares?	George Balanchine	George Gershwin, orchestrated by Hershy Kay	October 1992
Zirkus Weill	Kent Stowell	Kurt Weill/Norman Durkee	March 1989

PRINCIPAL
Patricia Barker
Anne Derieux
Paul Gibson
Linnette Hitchin
Ariana Lallone
Louise Nadeau
Jeffrey Stanton
Manard Stewart
Julie Tobiason
Ross Yearsley

PRINCIPAL CHARACTER
ARTIST
Uko Gorter
Flemming Halby
Victoria Pulkkinen

SOLOIST
Marisa Albee
Lisa Apple
Seth Belliston
Vladislav Bourakov
Vincent Cuny
Kimberly Davey
Alexandra Dickson
Konstantin Kouzin
Kaori Nakamura
Charles Newton
Melanie Skinner
Angela Sterling
Olivier Wevers

CORPS DE BALLET
Nicholas Ade
Joseph Anderson
Catherine Baker
Leah Belliston
Batkhurel Bold
Rachel Butler
Maria Chapman
Jeremy Conner
Natalia Haigler
Carrie Imler
Gavin Larsen
Timothy Lynch
Paige Parks
Brad Phillips
Jennifer Sax
Kim Smith
Jodie Thomas
John Todd
Patrick Tulleners
John Winfield
Astrit Zejnati

APPRENTICE
Maria Anderson
Angela Falivena
Noelani Pantastico
Steven Ruane
Scott Turner

PACIFIC NORTHWEST BALLET
FORMER DANCERS
*Listed by position at date of
leaving PNB*

PRINCIPAL
Albertson, Alaina	80-86
Annegarn, Steven	91-93
Auer, Michael	78-89
Bigney, Hugh	81-90
Carrabba, Marco	80-81
Davi, Brent	89-94
Ebitz, Gerard	85-86
Guillaumin, Sylvie	87-91
Hadley, Deborah	78-91
Hancock, Jory	78-82
Houk, Benjamin	83-96
Hughey, Lucinda	80-93
Lowe, Melissa	78-80
Mesnier, Michel	87-91
Messac, Magali	86-88
Miller, Adam	80-86
Neary, Colleen	86-92
Pasaric, Irena	82-84
Peck, Leslie	77-80
Reyes, Andre	93-96
Rotaru, Pavel	82
Rowe, Susan	80-85
Schwender, Jerry	77-80
Thordal-Christensen, Aage	86-92
Troy, Ellen	80-82
Walthall, Wade	82-88
Wivel, Ulrik	93-96

SOLOIST
Bronfman, Alejandra	84-90
Bruce, Cheryl	77-81
Clark, Harriet	86-92
Fischbach, Erica	86-94
Gladstone, Susan	85-92
Hecht, Bjarne	87-89
Heng Da, Li	90-96
Homme, Carey	81-88
Jones, Anthony	90-95
Kaiser, Kevin	82-95
Kekoa, Sterling	81-94
Mendes, Antonio	77-78
Miegge, Elisabeth	92-94
Mitchell, Kabby	78-84
Nieves, Dagoberto	89-94
Otto, Phillip	91-96
Peden, David	90-92
Pulkkinen, Victoria	81-83
Rohde, Lauri-Michelle	87-94
Rosal, Maia	81-88
Rose, Amy	92-97
Schwennesen, Don	82-84
Tardy, Alexandre	96-97
Tice, Ronn	86-91
Vise, Leslie	77-81
Xin, Yu	91-96

CORPS DE BALLET
Albertson, Jill	77-85
Alvarez, Alejandro	95-96
Alvarez, Raul	89-90
Andersen, Carol	83-87
Bail, Laura	78-82
Baird, Mark	78-82
Bauer, Ellen	87
Boyle, Martha	77-86
Brace, Dianne	85-88
Brackman, Kristen	89-97
Braman, Valeda	77-80
Britton, Barbara	90-91
Brown, Laura	80-82
Bullock, Jeffrey	86-90
Cederlund, Christian	84-88
Cederlund, Erik	86-87
Crawford, Rebecca	77-81
Damestoy, Irene	84-89
Donaldson, Carron	83-86
Doyle, Christopher	87-88
Erlon, Bernadette	77-78
Farris, Corey	79-80
Farruggio, Charles	90-94
George, Kristie	94-97
Gillenwater, Carlton	82-84
Goetz, Theresa	89-96
Greene, Amy	84-89
Greenwood, Rachel	93-94
Hall, Kathleen	77-78
Hogan, Anne	82-83
Homans, Jennifer	82-86
Horspool, Archie	78-81
Irwin, Stephanie	84-87
Jaffe, Bryce	89-93
Jones, James	80-81
Kenney, Christopher	88-91
Kerr, Maurya	88-90
Kipp, Lisa	85-86, 89-90
Kirkland, Ken	81-84
Kubeja, Clara Wilson	86-92
Leach, Barbara	77-78
Leuthauser, Martin	82-83
Lynch, Karen	89-93
May, Elizabeth	78-86
McCallister, Lisa	78-86
McCarthy, Elizabeth	83-87
McCready, Kathy	77-78
Meisenholder, Karen	87-93
Mele, April	77-78
Mraz, Ken	77-78
Musselman, Sean	85-86
Newton-Mason, Luke	90-91
Nugent, Dana	77-78
Olson, Reid	89-90
Parker, Kerry	89-92
Peltz, Elizabeth	78-81
Person, Phillip	77-78
Porter, Jennifer	86-89
Preston, Kay	85-86
Purvis, Cynthia	77-78
Qian Ping, Guo	91-92

Ray, Daniel	77-78
Rea, David	92-96
Renhard, Ann	83-86
Rice, Jacob	84-89
Robson, Jeanne	78-81
Roman, Christopher	90-92
Rouse, Cedric	89-91
Santillo, William	77-81
Santos, Lisa	80-81
Schneider, Phyllis	78-80
Schroeder, Noelle	92-94
Schwarz, Daniel	77-82
Schwenk, Laura	81-86
Smidt, Christopher	88-90
Spaight, Dennis	78-82
Stewart, Anne	77-78
Stickelman, Lisa	77-80
Stolzy, Lisa	78-90
Strang, Cynthia	86-87
Taylor, Laura	91-93
Thatcher, Ian	93-97
Thornburg, Valerie	80-81
Thouveny, Francoise	87-88
Torcicollo, Lisa	77-78
Vaillant, Lisl	86-87
Vercruysse, Luc	79-80
Vierthaler, Heidi	86-90
Villarini, Lisa	81-83
Vise, Misty	80-81
Weaver, Courtland	81-87
Williamson, Lisa	92-93
Wilson, Kate	82-85
Wong, Daniel	86-94
Woods, Robert	80-81

APPRENTICE
Balthrop-Lewis, Amara	92-93
Buie, Gigi	81-83
Gardner, Sally	82-83
Goldberg, Naomi	80-81
Goodman, Todd	84-85
Jones, Terace	88-89
Lowenberg, Stacy	94-96
Petta, Laura	81-82
Vendley, Michelle	93-94
Von Tobel, Valorie	96-97
Wayne, Taryn	96-97
Yaggi, Kirsten	91-92

PACIFIC
NORTHWEST
BALLET

ORCHESTRA

STEWART KERSHAW
*Music Director and
Principal Conductor*

ALLAN DAMERON
Associate Conductor

VIOLIN I
Marjorie Kransberg-Talvi
Concertmaster

John Pilskog
Associate Concertmaster

Linda Anderson
Lynn Bartlett-Johnson
Tom Dziekonski
Ella Marie Gray
Rebecca Lowe-Reed
Christine Olason
Marcia Ott
Arthur Zadinsky

VIOLIN II
Ingrid Frederickson
Principal

Bryan J. Boughten
William E. Boyd
Anne Cady
Stephen Daniels
Irwin Eisenberg
Philip Nation
Kim Zabelle

VIOLA
Leslie Johnson
Principal

Betty Agent
Timothy Hale
Joyce Ramee
Ruth Seraque
Eileen Swanson

CELLO
Page Smith
Principal

Meg Brennand
Andrea Chandler
Virginia Dziekonski
Gretchen Gettes
Rajan Krishnaswami

BASS
Ring Warner
Principal

Todd Larsen
Ben Musa
Stephen Schermer

FLUTE
Karla Flygare
Principal

Rae Terpenning

OBOE
Ove Hanson
Principal

Tad Margelli

CLARINET
Jennifer Nelson
Principal

Chris Inguanti

BASSOON
Mona Butler
Principal

Penny C. Lorenz

HORN
Rodger Burnett
Principal

Jean Bennett-Rynearson
Richard Reed
James Weaver

TRUMPET
George Oram
Principal

Richard Werner

TROMBONE
Mark Williams
Principal

Kay D. Nichols
Douglas Nierman

TUBA
Richard W. Byrnes

KETTLEDRUMS
Phillip Hanson

PERCUSSION
Matthew Kocmieroski
Principal

Michael A. Clark

HARP
Heidi Lehwalder

KEYBOARD
Dianne Chilgren
Allan Dameron

PERSONNEL MANAGER
Rodger Burnett

THERAPY & CONDITIONING
PROGRAM
Cynthia Jordan
Marjorie Thompson
Conditioning Staff

Karen Clippinger, M.S.P.E.
Program Consultant

Peter Shmock & Associates
*Injury Prevention & Strength
Development Program*

Seattle Sports Physical
Therapy
Physical Therapy Services
Boyd Bender
Carla Corrado
Physical Therapists

Steven Anderson, M.D.
Consulting Physician

Pierce E. Scranton Jr., M.D.
Consulting Physician

SPECIAL COUNSEL
Philip Morse,
Perkins Coie
Employment Law

Frank Retman,
MacDonald Hoague & Bayless
Immigration Law

PACIFIC NORTHWEST
BALLET SCHOOL
Francia Russell
Director

Paula Prewett
Principal

Denise Bolstad
School Administrator

Victoria Pulkkinen
Curriculum Supervisor

Julie Fuller
School Secretary

Wendy Casper
Administrative Assistant

Marsha Bennion
Administrative Assistant

Jodi Rea
Eastside Assistant

FACULTY
Sonia Dawkins
Sara deLuis
Flemming Halby
Dane Holman
Cynthia Jordan
Lucia Kuimova
Phillip Otto
Lisa Peterson
Victoria Pulkkinen
Stephanie Saland
Lynne Short
Abbie Siegel
Marjorie Thompson
Bruce Wells
Alice Yearsley

ACCOMPANISTS
Irv Huck
Principal Accompanist

Stephen Barnes
Vladimir Benenson
Carol Buschmann
Brian Chronister
Marleen Galvan
Elizabeth Hasse
Joan Havercroft
Pat Moskowitz
Katja Rubin
Paul Sklar
Nancy Slanina
Leona Troese
Don Vollema

CONSULTING STAFF
Toby Diamond, Ph.D.
Psychologist

Peggy Otto Swistak, M.S.,
R.D., C.D.
Nutritionist

Alan S. Woodle, D.P.M.
Podiatrist

*Stage Crew work is performed
by employees represented by
I.A.T.S.E. Local #15.*

*Wardrobe attendants provided
by members of Theatrical
Wardrobe Union #887,
I.A.T.S.E.*

*Stage draperies by I.Weiss &
Sons, Inc., New York.*

*Sherman Clay is the official
purveyor of pianos for PNB.*

*Pointe shoes exclusively by
Freed of London, Ltd.*

Deloitte & Touche, Auditors.

*Italic page numbers indicate
photographs.*